MASKING INEQUALITY WITH GOOD INTENTIONS

SYSTEMIC BIAS, COUNTERSPACES, AND DISCOURSE ACQUISITION IN STEM EDUCATION

PRACTICES & POSSIBILITIES

Series Editors: Aimee McClure, Mike Palmquist, and Aleashia Walton

Series Associate Editor: Jagadish Paudel

The Practices & Possibilities Series addresses the full range of practices within the field of Writing Studies, including teaching, learning, research, and theory. From Richard E. Young's taxonomy of "small genres" to Patricia Freitag Ericsson's edited collection on sexual harassment in the academy to Jessie Borgman and Casey McArdle's considerations of teaching online, the books in this series explore issues and ideas of interest to writers, teachers, researchers, and theorists who share an interest in improving existing practices and exploring new possibilities. The series includes both original and republished books. Works in the series are organized topically.

The WAC Clearinghouse and University Press of Colorado are collaborating so that these books will be widely available through free digital distribution and low-cost print editions. The publishers and the series editors are committed to the principle that knowledge should freely circulate and have embraced the use of technology to support open access to scholarly work.

RECENT BOOKS IN THE SERIES

Jessica Nastal, Mya Poe, and Christie Toth (Eds.), *Writing Placement in Two-Year Colleges: The Pursuit of Equity in Postsecondary Education* (2022)

Natalie M. Dorfeld (Ed.), *The Invisible Professor: The Precarious Lives of the New Faculty Majority* (2022)

Aimée Knight, *Community is the Way: Engaged Writing and Designing for Transformative Change* (2022)

Jennifer Clary-Lemon, Derek Mueller, and Kate Pantelides, *Try This: Research Methods for Writers* (2022)

Jessie Borgman and Casey McArdle (Eds.), *PARS in Practice: More Resources and Strategies for Online Writing Instructors* (2021)

Mary Ann Dellinger and D. Alexis Hart (Eds.), *ePortfolios@edu: What We Know, What We Don't Know, And Everything In-Between* (2020)

Jo-Anne Kerr and Ann N. Amicucci (Eds.), *Stories from First-Year Composition: Pedagogies that Foster Student Agency and Writing Identity* (2020)

Patricia Freitag Ericsson, *Sexual Harassment and Cultural Change in Writing Studies* (2020)

Ryan J. Dippre, *Talk, Tools, and Texts: A Logic-in-Use for Studying Lifespan Literate Action Development* (2019)

MASKING INEQUALITY WITH GOOD INTENTIONS

SYSTEMIC BIAS, COUNTERSPACES, AND DISCOURSE ACQUISITION IN STEM EDUCATION

By Heather M. Falconer

The WAC Clearinghouse
wac.colostate.edu
Fort Collins, Colorado

University Press of Colorado
upcolorado.com
Denver, Colorado

The WAC Clearinghouse, Fort Collins, Colorado 80523

University Press of Colorado, Denver, Colorado 80202

ISBN 978-1-64215-160-2 (PDF) | 978-1-64215-161-9 (ePub) | 978-1-64642-389-7 (pbk.)

DOI 10.37514/PRA-B.2022.1602

Produced in the United States of America

Library of Congress Cataloging-in-Publication Data

Names: Falconer, Heather M., 1974– author.
Title: Masking inequality with good intentions : systemic bias, counterspaces, and discourse acquisition in STEM education / by Heather M. Falconer.
Description: Fort Collins, Colorado : The WAC Clearinghouse ; Denver, Colorado : University Press of Colorado, [2022] | Series: Practices & possibilities | Includes bibliographical references
Identifiers: LCCN 2022052904 (print) | LCCN 2022052905 (ebook) | ISBN 9781646423897 (paperback) | ISBN 9781642151602 (adobe pdf) | ISBN 9781642151619 (epub)
Subjects: LCSH: Science—Study and teaching (Higher)—Social aspects—United States. | Mathematics—Study and teaching (Higher)—Social aspects—United States. | Discrimination in science—United States. | Sex discrimination in science—United States. | Discrimination in education—United States. | Sex discrimination in education—United States.
Classification: LCC Q182.8 .F35 2022 (print) | LCC Q182.8 (ebook) | DDC 507.1/1—dc23/eng20230123
LC record available at https://lccn.loc.gov/2022052904
LC ebook record available at https://lccn.loc.gov/2022052905

Copyeditor: Karen Peirce
Designer: Mike Palmquist
Cover Art: iStock Image 157680951 by Ugurhan Betin (www.instagram.com/ugurhan/)
Series Editors: Aimee McClure, Mike Palmquist, and Aleashia Walton
Series Associate Editor: Jagadish Paudel

The WAC Clearinghouse supports teachers of writing across the disciplines. Hosted by Colorado State University, it brings together scholarly journals and book series as well as resources for teachers who use writing in their courses. This book is available in digital formats for free download at wac.colostate.edu.

Founded in 1965, the University Press of Colorado is a nonprofit cooperative publishing enterprise supported, in part, by Adams State University, Colorado State University, Fort Lewis College, Metropolitan State University of Denver, University of Alaska Fairbanks, University of Colorado, University of Denver, University of Northern Colorado, University of Wyoming, Utah State University, and Western Colorado University. For more information, visit upcolorado.com.

Land Acknowledgment. The Colorado State University Land Acknowledgment can be found at landacknowledgment.colostate.edu.

Contents

Acknowledgments vii

Introduction 5

Chapter 1. The Intersection of Language, Culture, and Power 27

Chapter 2. Lifting the Curtain: Working With, and Against, White
Institutional Presence in Science 39

Chapter 3. The Psychosocial Costs of Race- and Gender-Evasive
Ideologies. 55

Chapter 4. Performing Race and Gender in Science 81

Chapter 5. Structuring Communities of Understanding and Support 107

Chapter 6. Building Equity with Counterspaces 117

References 131

Appendix. Methodological and Analytical Procedures 145

Acknowledgments

This book was written in the interstitial spaces that occurred over many, many years: on scraps of paper riding the Red Line and in phone dictation while commuting to campus, on paper copies flying in airplanes and in the mountains of Glencoe, in late-night bouts of insomnia and pre-dawn hours of inspiration, in the few hours between school drop-off and pick-up, the quiet of office hours, the marathon sessions during summer camp. Mothering as an early-career scholar has meant that neither being a mother nor being an academic has been done with any sense of normalcy. What normalcy *has* existed is due in large part to the generous and thoughtful people who have surrounded me and to whom I would like to give thanks.

Without my husband Iain's strength, support, patience, and flexibility, none of this would have happened. His personal and professional sacrifices have been immense, and for that I am both humbled and grateful. Without my son Lachlan's inquisitiveness and constant gaze, I might not have worked as hard or taken the opportunities that presented themselves. My fear of letting him down has helped me see that I have strengths beyond which I knew. Above all, he has reminded me to always, even in the hardest times, find something to laugh about. Without the sacrifices made by my mother, who left us way too early, the first two years of this scholarship would have been impossible to complete. Though we always envisaged she would be here to see the end product, I know that she is smiling from a distance. Finally, my brother and father have been a great source of support, reminding me of why I do the work I do.

My academic community has likewise been of enormous support and has helped to shape not only this work but my academic self, as well. Without the guidance and support of Neal Lerner, I am certain I would have been lost in a sea of data. His clarity and constant reassurance helped me find a path through and reminded me to trust my instincts when I was certain my instincts were wrong. For that, I am immeasurably grateful. Without the enthusiasm and encouragement of Mya Poe, I would not have realized that I could combine my love of writing with my love of science *and* social justice, and this project never would have happened. From our first conversation, she modeled the exact type of scholar I want to continue to be: forthright, dedicated, and rigorous without losing the essence of what this work is really about—people. And to Ellen Cushman, who taught me the first time we met just how important origin stories are. Without knowing *why* we do the work we do, without understanding where it comes from, it is too easy to lose sight of the end goal or sustain enthusiasm.

I want to thank Laura Proszak for always lending an ear and a message of support. Never underestimate the value of having someone with whom you can start a conversation with, "Can I get your opinion on something?" Thanks to David R.

Russell and Mary Lourdes Silva for their regular conversation and critical eye in our writing group; to Dylan Dryer, Ryan Roderick, Kevin Smith, Lindsay Illich, and Melissa Anyiwo for their thoughtful insights on chapters and consummate professionalism; to Melissa Jean-Charles for getting me away on writing retreats to rethink this book's structure and approach and to challenge my preconceptions of what it was supposed to look like. To Mike Palmquist, Aleashia Walton, Aimee McClure, and Jagadish Paudel for seeing the value of this work and publishing it in the Practices & Possibilities book series, and to the reviewers who offered such valuable insight into the text as a whole. So many have read and commented on this work over the years, and for that I am so grateful.

Last, but certainly not least, this work would not be possible without the students and faculty members who opened their lives to me. Their willingness to share their stories and work has meant that I can bring those experiences to light and, hopefully, help others. My gratitude goes out to the team at John Jay College and PRISM, with special thanks to Anthony Carpi and Edgardo Sanabria-Valentín for their on-site support of this research. Finally, I would like to thank the Conference on College Composition and Communication for recognizing this research with an Emergent Researcher Award and the mentorship of Dominic DelliCarpini. This research would have been hampered severely without their support.

MASKING INEQUALITY WITH GOOD INTENTIONS

SYSTEMIC BIAS, COUNTERSPACES, AND DISCOURSE ACQUISITION IN STEM EDUCATION

"What is the blood on the tracks that I happened to survive that others did not? My life experience tells me that when you don't find Blacks in the Sciences, when you don't find women in the Sciences . . . I know that these forces are real that I had to survive in order to get to where I am today."

~ Neil deGrasse Tyson (angetworld, 2014)

Introduction

Why Are You Here?

It's June 1991. I'm sitting in my high school guidance counselor's office trying to explain why I, a rising senior at a vocational-technical school, want permission to take the ninth-grade biology course at the adjacent high school during the coming year. Though the two schools are physically connected, the kids enrolled in vo-tech do not attend the same classes as the kids at Weymouth North. We do our week of shop (I am in a course called Graphic Arts, running offset printers and cameras larger than me), and then a week of watered-down, basic, lowest-level-to-graduate courses in math, English, and random electives. I have not had a high school science class for two years.

"A few months ago," my counselor comments, "you were talking about dropping out of school entirely and getting your GED. Now you want to take a class that doesn't fit into your curriculum and is going to take you out of shop for two hours each week?"

"Yes, that's correct."

"Why, again?" she asks, looking somewhat annoyed.

"Because I've been told by two college entrance advisors that I won't get accepted unless I take at least another science class." I have already told her this. I'm looking to her to help me navigate this space, but it is like pulling teeth. No one in my family attended college; my mother earned a bookkeeping certificate from a local community college when I was three, and my dad received his plumbing and HVAC licenses not long after they married. Outside of my mother and the college entrance advisors, I have spoken to no one in detail about my ambitions. When it was mentioned to my father, he stopped speaking to me for a few weeks until I remembered my "place."

The advisor looks at me and, in complete seriousness, says: "But Vokies don't go to college. You're preparing for the trades."

There is a clear message in her comment that I try to ignore. Those of us who are "Vokies" are there largely because we have not fit in at traditional schools for a wide variety of reasons: socioeconomic, ability, behavioral. Probably the only factor that few of us at this predominantly White school think about is race. As a White 16-year-old girl, it certainly escapes my notice because my attention is on the things that directly impact me. I leave the meeting not only feeling down but also with the reluctant concession of my counselor to sign off on the biology class if, and only if, my shop teacher *and* the biology teacher both agree. Neither my mother nor I mention this to my father.

~~~

Spring 1993: I'm a first-year college student in an introductory biology course. I sit toward the back left, furiously taking notes but also close to the door for an easy escape. This is my second attempt at the class because of an F the prior semester, which technically makes it the third biology class I have taken in my life. My professor, a man in his late 50s, stands at the board asking questions about the difference between mitosis and meiosis. Though other students raise their hands to answer, he calls on me. I know both processes relate to cell division, but I cannot remember off the top of my head which one does what. Afraid to answer incorrectly, I simply say, "I can't remember the difference." He smirks, then calls on someone else to answer.

At the end of that class, he asks me to stay back. He wants to know why I am at the college. He says that he notices how I am struggling to remember the concepts in the class; my test scores reflect poor comprehension. He feels that it might be a good idea for me to reconsider my major. Instead of ecology, maybe I should consider another major more suited to my skills. Maybe environmental education.

~~~

The following fall, I am enrolled in a wildlife biology course—a course I should not be in because I have not taken the second required biology course in the prerequisite sequence, but I do not know this, and no one caught it during registration. We are out in the deciduous forest of Central Maine learning how to tag and track large mammals. I have done the required readings, prepared myself for the lab, and am ready to apply the knowledge I have gathered over the past weeks. I have been showing up for myself and we are *finally* getting to do the work.

As one of two females in the class, I am by default put into a group with two male students. Our professor hands the radio equipment to one, the tracking gear to the other. To me, he hands a clipboard so that I can take notes.

In the 30 minutes we are working independently, it becomes clear that neither of my lab partners did their homework. Neither is prepared for the lab, yet neither will listen to my suggestions nor let me have a turn with the gear. They talk over me until our instructor comes back to evaluate our progress. We have accomplished nothing. We all receive a low score for lab work that day.

~~~

The following summer, I am sitting at a picnic table across from a senior environmental scientist I had met ten minutes prior. The late afternoon summer sun in Vermont makes everything look golden and ethereal. To my left are other undergraduates who have joined me at a summer institute to examine wetland ecology in New England. I worked extra hours during spring semester to afford the tuition, made the four-hour drive with $40 in my bank account to cover the gas here and back. I am here because I want to be. The other students chat comfortably with one another, as though they have known each other for years, not hours.

"What are your research interests?" the scientist across the table barks at me. Startled, I respond, "Oh! I, um, I'm studying ecology."

"Yes, but what are your *interests*? Why are *you* here?" His challenge has a tone that makes me physically recoil, a hostility that feels out of place and disorienting. My mind freezes, he loses patience, and then he stands with an irritation that others notice and moves to the other end of the table where the other, more chatty, students are. My feeling of not belonging has just been validated and publicly marked.

~~~

It's my final semester in college. Despite negative messaging along the way from both the faculty and my own family, I have managed to be on the dean's list for five semesters straight, compensating for my earlier poor academic performance. I have completed an undergraduate research project on red maples; navigated questionable encounters with male faculty that, today, would be clear violations of Title IX; and did not switch my major. I "persisted" and was "retained." I'm earning that Bachelor of Science degree in ecology and am very proud of myself.

As I prepare for leaving, though, I start to realize that there are no clear paths forward career-wise. I am only now learning about graduate school and have no idea about the processes and protocols associated with applying. Nor do I have the financial means to pay for applications or, should I be accepted, tuition. My boyfriend proposes, and the pressure to marry is strong despite it being a poor fit. Not knowing what I am supposed to do next, after graduation I fall into a series of jobs with environmental nonprofits, temporary employment agencies, and farms. I become an AmeriCorps VISTA member for two terms of service, hoping to pay down some of the school loans with which I have financed my education. I travel at the whim of my now-husband, looking for jobs throughout the US but ending up in low-paying, entry-level secretarial positions over and over again. When I *do* get around to applying to graduate programs, I learn that my 2.99 GPA is not good enough, that I do not have connections to faculty at any of the universities I want to attend, and that my recommenders' letters just cannot make up the difference to convince programs they should take me on. I end up working in environmental education after all.

~~~

These moments in my life as an undergraduate science student and college graduate are only a small handful of countless similar experiences. Yet, they illustrate the many ways that microaggressions toward women and first-generation students play out in educational spaces on a daily basis. They represent the regular messaging that women and other groups marginalized in STEM fields receive, telling them they do not belong. They show the ways in which programs do not think far enough ahead to what will happen when students *leave* academic institutions and encounter the "real" professional world.

It is easy to write these moments off as flukes, random anomalies that do not really represent what it is like to try to exist in a discipline that has historically kept people like you out. But when you live it, when those experiences recur with enough frequency that they are predictable, when you realize there is something more going on and feel the compounding effects of being told over and over and over again that you do not *quite* belong, that you are not *quite* the *right* fit—that takes its toll on both your psyche and your sense of self.

In their book *Race, Rhetoric, and Research Methods*, Alexandria L. Lockett and her coauthors (2021) note that, "when researching race and racism, one's relationship to the concepts should be identified" (p. 25). Our experiences and beliefs about race and racism—and gender, class, etc.—are intricately linked to how we as individuals are impacted by these various vectors of oppression. I have tried to begin that relationship identification with the vignettes shared from my early academic life, though I recognize their limitations.

I identify as a White, cis-female, heterosexual, first-generation college student from a working class background. I also have congenital hearing loss and other hidden disabilities that impact the way I interact with the world. My interest in race and racism is intertwined with my interest in gender, class, and ableness inequities (though these are *not* interchangeable—as Audre Lorde (1983) noted, "there is no hierarchy of oppressions;" they are unique forces unto themselves). While I recognize that this explicit positioning can look like virtue signaling or performative allyship, I push back, here, to argue that *not* acknowledging my positionality as a researcher does more to hide any bias than to reveal it. In fact, providing this orientation allows you, the reader, to contextualize my findings and interpretations in more meaningful ways. As Lockett, et al. (2021) have argued passionately, to not acknowledge this positioning is to make race, racism, class, gender, ability, etc., invisible. Origin stories matter. Research is personal.

The questions explored in this book, in many ways, were seeded in my own struggle to become a recognized scientist. As a low-income female at an expensive private college, my attempts to acculturate into the field of science were disrupted by my own underpreparedness, male professors who did not see women as belonging in the field, and an inability (because of financial resources) to participate in the many extracurricular activities that led to job placement and graduate school acceptance (i.e., unpaid internships). At the time, of course, I did not recognize this disruption as something outside of my own skills and abilities. Instead, I saw these as evidence of my inability to "do science." Some of my professors at the time claimed that I (and women generally) lacked the rigor and grit to do this kind of work. With time and life experience, however, I came to recognize that my inability to acculturate and make a career in science was similar to many others' and that it was not entirely in my control. The "pull yourself up from the bootstraps" (Villanueva, 1993) mentality that permeates American society is fraught with tensions and obstacles that are rarely explicitly addressed by and with those whom they most powerfully affect.

In 2009, I took on the role of science grants and projects administrator for the Research Foundation of the City University of New York system. Placed at John Jay College of Criminal Justice (John Jay), the largest four-year Hispanic-serving institution (HSI) in the Northeast, I was tasked with helping to build capacity for academic programs in science that served students much like myself. Though most of these students identified as part of Latinx, African American, and Asian American communities and encountered societal challenges that I did not experience because of my Whiteness, many of them were women, as I am, and almost all of them came from low-income households, as I did. These were students who, as I had, worked part- or full-time jobs to pay for tuition, housing, and food. They juggled family commitments and expectations with the rigor of an academic discipline with specific modes of communicating and expectations for participation. They were trying to negotiate membership in a new community with very specific ways of being, thinking, and knowing while keeping one or both feet rooted in the communities that raised and supported them. The difference between us, however, was that they were making it work. They were figuring out how to become recognized members of the scientific community, publishing papers and moving on to postgraduate programs in various scientific fields.

As part of my professional role with the college, I designed and participated in assessment practices that would help me and my colleagues not only report back to our granting agencies on project success but also offer insight into the initiatives that were having a real impact on student persistence and growth. We examined the various initiatives through the lens of Vincent Tinto's (1993) framework of social and academic integration, showing how the institutionalization of the initiatives supported student success throughout their collegiate experience (Carpi et al., 2013), as well as through social cognitive career theory to examine how the undergraduate research experience affected career choice (Carpi et al., 2017). Through all of this research, however, it felt like the individual student experiences were being lost (focusing instead on measurable metrics like GPA and graduate program placement), and the role of reading, writing, speaking, and listening was left unexamined.

As has been demonstrated by Jean Lave and Etienne Wenger (1991), Wenger (1998), Dorothy A. Winsor (1996), Anne Beaufort (2007), and others, acculturating into a community of practice involves adopting the ways of being, thinking, and knowing of the community. Included in these ways are the communicative practices—the discourse conventions (Swales, 1990)—that help members of the community recognize other members of the community. During my time with the program, I was impressed at how students could enter with what some considered poor writing skills (I was not privy to their reading skills) yet graduate with publications to their name. I wondered whether they were being explicitly taught the discourse conventions of their discipline, or if their mentors simply carried them along in the writing aspects of science (e.g., providing preconstructed data sheets to fill out or proposal text to revise). I wondered whether students' prior knowledge about science and the genres common to the scientific community helped or hindered their development as scientific writers and whether their identities as female, BIPOC[1], or low-income students permeated this writing and was revealed or suppressed. To that end, this research project was born.

The findings in this book are the result of an in-depth, longitudinal case study of the Program for Research Initiatives in Science and Math (PRISM), a unique undergraduate research program housed within John Jay. What makes this program particularly interesting is not simply its structure (it conducts real-world research in physical and computer sciences) but also that a significant portion of the students participating in it are women of color—predominantly Black and Latinx, populations largely underserved in higher education.[2] Further, since its inception in 2006, the program has had great success in placing students in graduate programs (particularly PhD, MD, and MPh programs)—something that was virtually unheard of for graduates of the forensic science major before PRISM's creation. In more recent years, the number of Research-1 institutions accepting PRISM students has also increased, likely a result of the professionalization that occurs as part of the program (e.g., publishing research and presenting at scientific conferences).

My orientation as a researcher of this particular program proved itself to be valuable. What people do—and what people hear and see—as researchers is dictated by what they are *able* to do, what they are *able* to hear and see, based not only on training but also on prior life experiences. It is also dictated by access to data. My experience as a "failed" female scientist meant that not only could I relate to many of the challenges my research participants disclosed, but I could also share some of my own, relevant experiences to create a richer dialogue and, in many cases, build stronger relationships. These relationships allowed for greater depth and nuance. Similarly, while I feel confident that the female research participants in this study were comfortable discussing their experiences of gender in science with me, I am equally confident that my Whiteness placed limitations on what participants felt comfortable sharing when discussing issues of race and racism. To pretend that I could fully understand what those experiences felt like would be disingenuous. As a result, I have worked hard to let participants' voices speak for themselves and to make clearly distinct the conclusions that I drew from observation and the conclusions that I drew based on participants' experiences and

---

1.   While there is no perfect way to discuss and define groups of people based on race/ethnicity, I have opted to use BIPOC in this text. BIPOC is the currently preferred acronym to identify individuals who are Black, Indigenous, or People of Color. This acronym, which can be used as either a noun or adjective, is more inclusive than the term People of Color because it recognizes the different oppressions different racial groups experience. I have been conscious, however, to use specific identifiers like Black and Latinx when specifically discussing an individual's experience.

2.   In the 2015–2016 academic year, 70 percent of PRISM students and 38 percent of faculty mentors identified as female; 78 percent of students and 38 percent of faculty mentors identified as Black, Latinx, or Asian.

claims. I have consciously not imposed ideas of intent by any party, rather reporting the events of given moments and the subsequent effects on students' reported experiences. Similarly, I have worked hard not to explain those experiences away with White privilege (McIntosh, 1989) or fragility (DiAngelo, 2018). I embrace and acknowledge that, in the US, Whiteness and patriarchy directs all that we do and see.

Study Purpose and Design

The research presented in this book comes from a larger in-depth, longitudinal, qualitative case study of PRISM, which received Institutional Review Board approval by both the Research Foundation of CUNY and Northeastern University. Begun in fall 2015 and continuing through spring 2019, the larger project sought to understand the ways in which students from underrepresented backgrounds in STEM negotiated disciplinary discourse conventions in an undergraduate research experience (URE) and the impacts of those negotiations on scientific identities. Some of the questions explored included examining the role of prior knowledge in the development of identity, the impact of mentors on learning and belonging, the understanding of scientific genres over time, the impact of program requirements and expectations, and the role of societal markers (i.e., race, gender, socioeconomic class) on identity development. The last two questions are the ones this book primarily addresses: How do the norms and expectations of higher education and, specifically, STEM education impact the development of scientific identity and discursive skill? What role do societal markers like race and gender play in the negotiation of identity in STEM learning environments?

While this project to some extent adopted ethnographic and grounded theory methods in the pursuit of answering these questions, the in-depth case study was selected as the methodology that best suited the study overall. As Robert E. Stake (1981) argues, case study research yields knowledge different from other qualitative methodologies—it is more concrete, resonating with our own experiences rather than being abstract; is rooted in context, where lived knowledge is distinguishable from abstract, formal knowledge of other designs; is more developed by reader interpretation; and is based more in reference populations determined by the reader than through generalizations (pp. 35–36). It is also a fitting construct for examining intersectional identities at work. This approach allowed me to make connections between actions and events that repeatedly occurred in the research program (i.e., proposal deadlines, symposium presentations) and the writing and speaking produced by participants. It also allowed me to chronicle how these factors interacted with and influenced participants' thinking about their discursive practice, their actual discursive development, and their identities as scientists. My interest was focused on how these participants were experiencing the world of the research program and how these experiences were influencing the ways in which they identified as scientists in reading, writing, speaking, and listening. By studying individual students within a "real-life, contemporary bounded system [(i.e., their laboratory and the program as a whole)] . . . over time, through detailed, in-depth data collection involving multiple sources of information," I was able to get an understanding of how individuals border-cross discourses and adopt or incorporate identities (Cresswell, 2013, p. 97).

Because of the nature of longitudinal work (i.e., the time and labor involved) and the potential intrusiveness on students and mentors, I designed this study to capitalize on the work already being conducted within the UREs. I attempted to make the project as unobtrusive as possible by observing the normal, regular interactions between students and their mentors and between students and program staff as they engaged in discursive tasks associated with their work in the undergraduate research program. To accomplish this goal, my project used semi-structured qualitative interviews with individuals participating in PRISM (students, mentors, and staff), the collection of writing that students completed as part of their PRISM work (including feedback provided by mentors and staff), the review of existing PRISM archival data (writing, questionnaires, surveys, etc.), and the observation of program training sessions and meetings related to discursive practices. Though I had originally planned to observe students and mentors within the laboratories, this proved impossible due to time—students and mentors were often in the labs at odd and unpredictable times of day, making the observation of numerous individuals virtually impossible to plan.

I transcribed and coded interviews, using Johnny Saldaña's (2015) work as a guide and emergent thematic coding (Boyatzis, 1995) to pull out common themes. I likewise coded written artifacts for rhetorical elements (e.g., hedges) and pedagogical moments (e.g., explicit instruction through feedback). I used existing archival data, such as surveys and questionnaires, to provide insight on the program as a whole as well as on student and mentor participants. Finally, direct observation provided insight into the instructional dynamic of formal program initiatives (such as creating posters or writing proposals). Combined, these streams of data allowed me to understand the various ways students were experiencing the program and the kinds of instruction being provided. The Appendix provides additional insight into my methodological and analytical procedures.

I selected participants through mass recruitment of both PRISM-enrolled students and PRISM faculty mentors to get as broad a pool as possible in terms of gender, race, and socioeconomic class. In the end, the participants that completed the study were an accurate representation of the program's student population as a whole. The project began with 11 students (I accepted all who responded to my call for participants), though attrition over time meant that I was able to collect complete data on only six. I asked students to share files of their writing with me in whatever form was most convenient. Most shared Google Docs, though a few simply emailed drafts multiple times throughout the semester. All students were compensated with a $50 gift card for each interview conducted (typically once per semester) and were given opportunities to review transcripts as well as to member-check my analysis and presentation of their experience. I also invited faculty mentors and program staff to participate, but I did not make them aware of whether any of their mentees were participants. Except in the case of Ruben, who chose to tell his mentor he was involved, none of the student participants were disclosed to their mentors. Interviews with mentors occurred once per semester, though mentors were not compensated for their time. Because of the highly specific nature of the work students did in their UREs, I have opted to minimize the use of textual artifacts in this text, opting instead to share quotations when relevant. Likewise, all participants were assigned pseudonyms and some identifying characteristics have been altered. These practices aid in maintaining participant anonymity as much as possible, though I made participants aware that I could not guarantee full anonymity.

Equity and STEM

In the United States, retention in STEM disciplines has been a topic of concern for decades. Just a few of the many initiatives aimed at making these fields more accessible to women, BIPOC, and individuals from low socioeconomic backgrounds include the U.S. Department of Education's Title V funding initiative, which focuses on improving higher education for Latinx students (with an emphasis on STEM) (Institutional Service, 2022); the Minority Science and Engineering Improvement Program, which supports activities that will build capacity for scientific and technological advancements by increasing the numbers of prepared underrepresented minorities in STEM (Institutional Service, 2021); and the Obama Administration's STEM for All program (launched in 2016), which argued that "every American student deserves access to a high-quality education in STEM for both their future and for the Nation's future" (Handelsman & Smith, para. 1). Yet, despite efforts like these, the STEM disciplines have proven to be remarkably resistant to changes in gender, racial, and socioeconomic demographics.

Data from the National Center for Science and Engineering Statistics (2019) illustrates this inertia. In 2006, there were over 478,000 bachelor's degrees awarded to undergraduates in science and engineering in the United States. Of those, seven percent were awarded to students identifying as Latinx, eight percent to those identifying as Black, and 50 percent to those identifying as female. By 2016, the overall number of degrees awarded to Latinx students increased 133 percent, to Black students 36 percent, and to women 37 percent—yet the overall *proportion* of the 2016 science and engineering graduating class had moved little. Of the 666,157 degrees awarded, Latinx students represented 13 percent (an improvement of six percentage points from ten years earlier), the percentage of Black students had not changed at all, and women had dropped 0.4 of a point to 49.6 percent. Women who identified as Black or Latinx comprised nine percent of all degrees awarded in 2006, but only 12 percent ten years later. These statistics reflect that, though overall enrollment in STEM fields has steadily increased, the relative proportion of different demographic groups has remained largely the same (Figure 1). Further, claims made by the Cooperative Institutional Research Program in 2010 remain true today: while underrepresented racial minorities "have reached parity with their White and Asian American counterparts in terms of their proportional interest in majoring in STEM disciplines at the beginning of their undergraduate studies" (para. 5), the disparity in completion rates and postgraduate study across races remains substantial. Statistics like these force us to look deeper: If interest in STEM and access to programming are not a factor, what is keeping so many underrepresented minorities out of STEM fields?

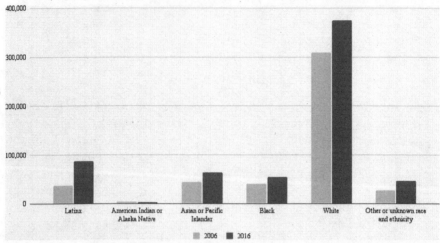

Figure 1. Science and Engineering Bachelor's Degrees Awarded by Race/Ethnicity (2006 vs. 2016). Despite student interest in STEM majors growing, discrepancies persist. The overall distribution of degrees awarded by race/ethnicity have stayed relatively static. Data from Table 5-3: Bachelor's degrees awarded, by field, citizenship, ethnicity, and race: 2006–16, by National Center for Science and Engineering Statistics, National Science Foundation, March 8, 2019 (https:// ncses.nsf.gov/pubs/nsf19304/assets/data/tables/wmpd19-sr-tab05-004.pdf).

Part of the problem, as Wendy Faulkner (2011) notes in her discussion of disparities in engineering, is that both research into gender- and race-based differences and the solutions posed tend to focus on deficits in underrepresented groups rather than deficits in the discipline (p. 278). In educational research, disparities have been attributed to a number of factors: familial responsibilities; a lack of academic mentorship; a need for a community of peers; and the missing experience of succeeding in self-directed, academic endeavors (Arana et al., 2011). Though disparities have also been attributed to cultural conflict in the classroom as a result of White, European educational frameworks (Delpit, 2006; Gay, 2010) as well as the marginalizing rhetoric of scientific discourse (Bonilla-Silva, 2018; Kahle, 1988; Kelly, 1985; Lederman, 1992; Mason et al., 1991; Torres, 2013; Yager &

Yager, 1985), few initiatives seek to remediate these barriers in educational spaces. Educational approaches have tended, instead, to focus on improving access to programs, particularly undergraduate research and bridge initiatives aimed at remediating math and reading skills.

This book flips the focus and instead explores the impact of systemic prejudice and bias on underrepresented students entering STEM disciplines, as well as offers solutions to rectify those impacts. It examines the lived experiences of individuals as they negotiate identities as members of scientific fields within an undergraduate research program at a HSI and how those experiences mediate disciplinary discourse acquisition. While the examination of identity and literacy is not new to writing studies (e.g., Burgess & Ivanič, 2010; Casanave, 2002; Gee, 2000), what I am interested in with this research are the large and small moments in the process of learning both a new disciplinary practice and a new discourse that disrupts or encourages knowledge and language acquisition. Representation, microaggressions, and preparedness can impact students as they consider future career-selves; mentor expectations, pedagogical approaches, and institutional climate can affect them once enrolled in college or university. This book explores these factors as experienced by six students engaged in undergraduate research in biological, chemical, and computer sciences—students from largely first-generation populations and considered racial and/or gender minorities within STEM fields due to underrepresentation. This book also offers a way of thinking about mentor-mentee interactions in practice by examining writing development in relation to identity and recognizing "the central role of power relations in literacy practices" (Street, 2001, p. 430).

Introduction to the Research Site and Student Participants

The research site discussed in this project is a unique one that speaks directly to many of the inequalities noted in the previous sections. A four-year public institution located in a large, urban city, John Jay has been recognized as the largest Hispanic-serving institution (HSI) in the Northeast, as well as designated a Minority-serving institution (MSI) (John Jay College on the Move, 2006). According to the college's Office of Institutional Research (2015), of the total undergraduates enrolled at the institution during this study period, 45 percent identified as Latinx, 22 percent as Black, 10 percent as Asian, and 23 percent as White (Native American, Pacific Islander, and Native Alaskan students constituted less than one percent of the student body); further, 41 percent of undergraduates were first-generation college students; 49 percent came from homes earning $30,000 or less per year; and 58 percent worked (many full-time) while taking classes.

The institution also houses an established science program that has grown in popularity over the years. In the mid-1990s, nationwide enrollment in STEM programs—and degrees awarded—began to rise (National Center for Science and Engineering Statistics, n.d.). While the institution's science program was no exception with regard to enrollment, attrition rates from the major suggested that the infrastructure and support systems in place at the institution were inadequately supporting the rapidly-rising population (Carpi et al., 2013b) (see Figure 2). Further, when comparing graduation rates of minority students to non-minority students by cohort, there was a clear discrepancy between the two groups in terms of attrition (see Figure 3). The cause of this discrepancy was not immediately apparent, but it was understood that a first step toward remediating it could be relationship-building through mentorship opportunities. Interestingly, statistics based on sex favored female students, with consistently higher female enrollments and graduation rates (see Figure 4).

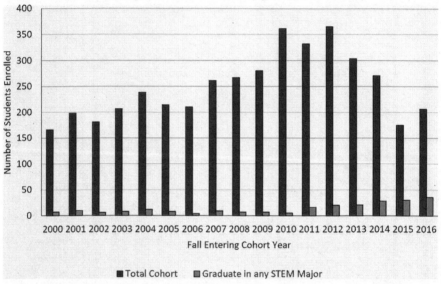

Figure 2. Enrollment in STEM Majors at John Jay College of Criminal Justice versus Degrees Awarded. Despite high enrollments in STEM majors, graduation rates remain disproportionately low. UREs through PRISM, however, have had a noticeable effect on graduation rates since 2011. Data provided through personal correspondence with PRISM, John Jay College of Criminal Justice, October 6, 2021.

Until the late 1990s, the institution offered its undergraduate students the opportunity to learn laboratory skills within the confines of specific courses and an external internship only; the support system for undergraduate research was lacking, active mentorship between faculty and student was rare, and students were exposed minimally, if at all, to basic scientific research (Carpi et al., 2013a). As the struggle to retain students in the science major became more and more apparent, so also did the expectations and aspirations of students who were successful academically. The proportion of students pursuing graduate school was miniscule; most saw the program as vocational training and considered their next logical step to be an entry-level job placement as a technician in a crime laboratory.

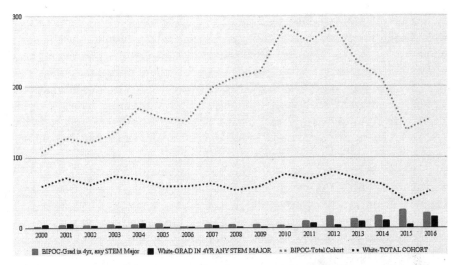

Figure 3. Aggregated BIPOC Enrollment and Graduates versus White Enrollment and Graduates in STEM Majors at John Jay College of Criminal Justice (by Year). PRISM was created in 2006, after which students slowly began engaging in undergraduate research and graduation rates for all students began to increase. Data provided through personal correspondence with PRISM, John Jay College of Criminal Justice, October 6, 2021.

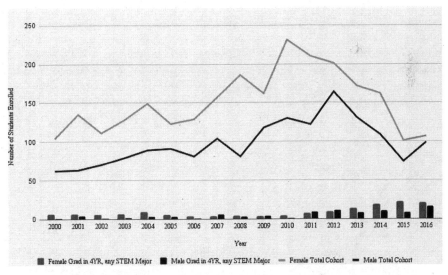

Figure 4. Graduation and Enrollment Numbers, by Cohort, Aggregated by Sex (Male versus Female). PRISM UREs have had a noticeable impact on graduation rates for both sexes, but particularly for students identifying as female. Data provided through personal correspondence with PRISM, John Jay College of Criminal Justice, October 6, 2021.

Junior and senior forensics students were failing to see themselves as scientists, capable of getting postgraduate degrees, or even to see where such degrees could lead them. As a result, a small group of faculty within the Department of Science recognized the potential to create opportunities that would increase student understanding of what it means to have a career in the sciences, feel part of the academic and scientific community, and actively engage with the scientific process. It was believed that by increasing opportunities for mentorship and social connections as well as by building an academic support framework, upper-level students would be more engaged, and the institution would see higher incidences of academic success in STEM, including an increase in women and students of color going on to postgraduate programs leading to high-level careers. The interventions instituted and their effects on retention have been well-documented elsewhere (see Carpi et al., 2013b). The intervention that is relevant to this research project, however, is the undergraduate research program.

The Program for Research Initiatives in Science and Math (PRISM)—which is unique among HSIs and MSIs—was formally begun in 2006 to provide opportunities for students in the science major to gain research experience that would prepare them for graduate programs in the sciences. The pedagogical goals in creating the program were three-fold: (a) to facilitate the engagement of students with the forensic science curriculum so as to assist their passage through the major; (b) to increase graduate/professional school acceptance rates and career success for graduates; and (c) to assist in the creation of a professional community that would extend beyond the students' years at the institution (Carpi et al., 2013a). In order to accomplish these goals, the program recognized that a multifaceted approach was necessary to increase interest in and motivation for STEM-related academic career paths among students. Science students are welcome to become participants in the URE program as early as their freshman year—including those who are attending classes with community college partners. This participation, however, is scaffolded based on academic standing—calculated by both completed coursework and grade point average. The only prerequisite is that they "should be planning a major in either forensic science or computer science and have some interest in possibly pursuing an advanced degree after obtaining their [Bachelor's]" (PRISM, 2016, n.p.). Student participation during their early years of college is limited to monthly meetings, where they can speak to other science students and hear presentations from professionals in the field, and enrichment activities such as program outings.

Once students have reached a stage in their academic career where they have declared their major in forensic science, have completed Organic Chemistry, earned a minimum GPA of 2.5, demonstrated proficiency in all science and math courses, and can show a sincere interest in attending graduate or medical school, they are invited to submit an application to participate in undergraduate research. Admittedly, this serves a gatekeeping function that some worthy students are unable to pass. Accepted students then take part in a one-week faculty-led research-training course. Topics include safe laboratory techniques, composing literature reviews, and the research proposal writing process. Applicants to the program then identify their areas of research interest and meet with potential mentors. While some students shadow others in the lab for a semester, others opt to write a research proposal immediately. This proposal is designed with the intended mentor's laboratory focus in mind and is unique to each student. It requires considerable thought on the student's part about a testable hypothesis, clear testing design, and appropriate timeframe for the semester in which they are working. If a student's proposal is accepted, they sign a contract of participation and are awarded a stipend commensurate with the number of hours they intend to conduct research. Those students who opt to only shadow others are not awarded a stipend but are able to submit a research proposal during the next cycle.

This scaffolded entry process reflects the principles and considerations used throughout the program's design. Students are not assumed by the program to possess a particular threshold of prior knowledge, experience, or motivation with research before applying (Deci & Ryan, 1985). While students enter the program with a wide array of background knowledge and experience, this programmatic approach allows for the broadest access possible. As such, the program does not assume that students are aware of research opportunities or of how participating in research could affect their future career paths. Though it does maintain a high standard for admittance, the program also provides support in meeting those standards, both through academic support (Carpi et al., 2013b) and preparation for the application process itself (i.e., research training course). Active recruitment through guest presentations in science courses maximizes student participation, especially among historically underrepresented student groups.

Once formally admitted to the program, new students also participate in an entry process specific to their mentors. While entry rituals vary depending on the area of research and the size and structure of the research group, each mentor has developed a routine that familiarizes a student with the people, equipment, and content related to the mentor's research. These routines include in-depth tours of the laboratories, reading lists of journal publications to orient students to the research being conducted, orientation to the equipment and processes used, and meetings with other students.

In addition to the lab's research-group community and the overall program community, faculty-mentored research also inculcates students into the broader community and culture of scientists in each field. As is necessary in a community of practice, faculty-mentored research reproduces knowledge in the form of scientific publications and reinforces the idea that publishing is a form of currency—that in order to acquire funding, one must be actively engaged with discussions taking place in the community. Introducing students to the economic and political facets of scientific research makes the end goal of publication clear. It also legitimizes program requirements such as the proposal process, which mimics the proposal process for actual grants. Familiarizing students with the ways in which professional scientists create and disseminate knowledge prepares them to be more self-sufficient researchers.

A distinct feature of a community of practice is its particular manner and style of discourse. As Lave & Wenger (1991) explain, "learning to become a legitimate participant in a community involves learning how to talk (and be silent) in the manner of full participants" (p. 105). The academic science community has its own practices and venues for the exchange of ideas and the reproduction of knowledge, such as scientific conferences and academic journal publications. PRISM provides scaffolded experiences for students to build towards these authentic practices, such as internal proposal submissions for continued funding as well as an annual on-campus research symposium where students create and present posters of their work. To prepare for these opportunities, students develop skill in scientific writing and presentation. Regular lab meetings provide an informal forum to regularly rehearse presentation skills and receive feedback. In addition to working with their mentors, students meet as a group for practice presentations and seminars on a variety of topics.

Beyond the internal events, the program also encourages students to participate in outside research events, including attending and presenting at academic conferences, participating in summer research programs, and submitting to undergraduate and professional journals. Mentors encourage students to engage in the discourse of the broader scientific community, lighting the path for their students. Additionally, the program's research training coordinator provides individualized guidance to students about applying to graduate programs. This guidance includes assistance with application requirements (such as writing personal statements), preparation for taking the Graduate Record Examination, requests for references, and other relevant matters.

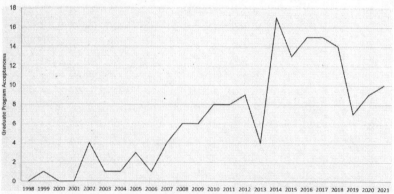

Figure 5. Number of PRISM Students Pursuing MD, PhD, and MD/PhD Degrees Over Time (Self-Declared). 1998 marked the start of informal research mentoring with a select group of students (4)—all of whom went on to PhD programs in 2002; 2006 marked the start of the formal URE program. Data provided through personal correspondence with PRISM, John Jay College of Criminal Justice, October 6, 2021.

As such, the program takes responsibility for guiding students through the formal structures and timelines associated with admissions to graduate institutions, which might otherwise be barriers to students, especially first-generation college students (Saunders & Serna, 2004). As Figure 5 reflects, the research program has had a marked effect on graduate school enrollments in professional research and academic tracks.

For the study being discussed here, my goal was in part to tease out how the social interaction between student researcher and mentor, as well as between students within the laboratory, shaped the student participants' individual realities with regard to reading and writing in scientific disciplines. This examination extended to their perspectives on the process of learning to write as a scientist as well as connections to identity. I was also concerned with interrogating disciplinary structures and practices with regard to systemic inequities, unpacking how these are enacted by even the most well-meaning individuals.

Student Participant Biographies

This research study collected complete data on six student participants at the research site over the course of four years (incomplete data was collected on another five).

Ruben was among the first students interviewed for this project. We began working together in the fall of 2015 after he had completed the required research training workshop during the summer. A first-generation college student, Ruben was in his mid-twenties, a father to a young child, and paying his own way through college by working in construction 30 hours per week. He identified as Latinx, having moved to the US from Central America at the age of ten. Though English was his second language, he read, wrote, and spoke both English and Spanish fluently. Ruben was pursuing a forensic science degree with an emphasis on toxicology. His hope was to finish his degree and secure a position in a criminalistics laboratory.

Ruben had no prior experiences with science as a career, nor with any members of his extended family pursuing higher education in general. Though there was support for this pursuit from family (i.e., his mother provided childcare during classes and work), he also experienced pushback from friends and family about his career aspirations, as they questioned his loyalty to his community and culture.

Natalia joined this research project in September 2016. She was 18 at the time; a sophomore forensic science student who had yet to decide on a track—though she was leaning more toward criminalistics than toxicology or molecular biology. When I asked her how she identified ethnically, Natalia hesitated. "There's always like two choices," she explained. "I usually check 'Hispanic slash Latino,'" explaining that she deferred to whatever option "on the form" was closest to this category. Spanish was her first language, but she was fluent and comfortable in both Spanish and English.

Natalia came to the college from an inner-city high school that focused specifically on STEM through health and human services. Her high school was also part of an initiative to provide early college exposure to students historically underrepresented at the collegiate level. As will be discussed, the opportunities provided through this high school initiative became important factors in developing Natalia's prior knowledge of research practices and scientific writing. Though as an adolescent and young adult she thought she would be a detective, her time at this high school introduced her to a variety of advanced sciences and research, including forensic science. The interest this piqued in Natalia caused her to seek out additional opportunities, including a forensics course offered to the students at the high school through a partnership with a state university as well as a research course focused specifically on the sciences.

Other than this early experience, Natalia had no direct exposure to scientists in her friend or family network. Science was simply a passion that was ignited and fostered through her educational experiences. Natalia had a strong family network, including significantly younger brothers and an older sister, who supported her in pursuing opportunities.

Chloe was also among the earliest participants to join the study. A young woman who identified as White, Chloe came from a low-income family in a small town two hours from New York City. She commuted by bus to and from the college four-to-five days per week, occasionally spending a night at a friend's apartment when possible. Chloe's family was very conservative and economically minded. There was significant pressure from her father, a car mechanic, and mother, a hair stylist, to earn a degree that would lead to a well-paying job. The men in Chloe's family also had strong opinions about the roles of women in society, often questioning her desire to become educated rather than marry and start a family. In addition to these challenges, Chloe was diagnosed with a severe anxiety disorder that had tangible impacts on her progression through college. The anxiety interfered with test-taking, composing high-stakes documents, and the ability to interact with those she saw as superior. It also impacted the options she saw for her future career.

Amrita joined the study in January 2016. A young woman of Indian decent (first generation American), she grew up in a relatively homogenously White suburban area in the Southern US before moving to the Northeast for school. She was raised in a middle-class family and attended a high school offering an International Baccalaureate program, of which she was a participant. Both of Amrita's parents are practicing physicians, which had interesting effects on her career choices and professional identity (as will be seen later). Her parents were enthusiastic about her educational decisions and supportive of her choice to move over 800 miles from home. Amrita's undergraduate education was financed largely by her parents, though her acceptance into a prestigious scholarship program provided academic assistance and opportunities for study abroad and internships. Though she was far away from her familial support network, Amrita quickly secured a community of friends through the college and her temple who shared both her social justice ideology and her drive toward professionalism. This network provided an important social structure that helped with networking as well as stamina.

From our first interaction, Amrita presented herself as a high-achieving, self-confident young woman; she was extremely articulate and formal in our written and spoken interchanges, with a strong sense of personal agency when it came to her extracurricular activities. This academic identity was reinforced by her position in the scholars' program and her successes as an undergraduate up to that point.

Anne also joined the study in January 2016. A young woman originally from South America, Anne self-identified as African American. Though she claimed to be relatively unfocused prior to college—her professional interests ranged from modeling to photography, ballerina to veterinarian—Anne was directed enough in her schooling not only to attend the top high school in her district but also to center her academics on science as well. Anne's schooling was based on the British system, where students take all subjects for the first three years, then begin to "stream" according to career desires and aptitude. Anne earned her "O-levels"[3] in biology, chemistry, and physics. Rather than continue into the more advanced "A-levels," which are prerequisites for attending university in the British system, Anne chose to leave school at 16 and move to the United States with her mother. Because of the differences in the schooling systems, Anne's mother wanted her to repeat high school in the US, but Anne resisted, agreeing only to "redo it" if she was not accepted into college. Her acceptance into John Jay ensured that she would not need to "backtrack."

Inspired by female scientists in television shows like *CSI* and *Dr. G Medical Examiner*, Anne came to the college to study forensic science with the hope of becoming a medical examiner. Though she was enthusiastic about pursuing this degree and what it might mean in terms of contributing to the world, Anne did absorb some of her mother's concerns that she might not be ready for the academic work—a doubt that persisted even after her success in coursework.

Finally, **Madalyn** was a woman in her early thirties pursuing a second bachelor's degree. She was raised in a middle-class family of Scandinavian descent ("super-White," as she joked in our first conversation) and, like many of the students I encountered at John Jay, was self-financing her education. Originally from New England, she came to New York City after earning a bachelor's in design elsewhere. After working in the art industry for a number of years, she decided to make a career shift and began taking classes in physical anthropology at another institution within the CUNY system. After finding the course offerings less than

---

3. O-levels are the equivalent of general requirements to graduate high school in the United States. A-levels are on par with Advanced Placement coursework, though slightly more rigorous.

what she was hoping for, she transferred to the forensic science program at John Jay in 2014. She joined the study in February 2016.

From our first encounter, Madalyn identified herself as a competent writer. She referenced her time working in a New York City art gallery, where she assisted in editing press releases and putting together art catalogs, as one example of the "different areas" she had worked in—professions that required "a certain kind of language." She presented a keen awareness of language and tone with respect to disciplinarity, and it became apparent in that first conversation that Madalyn possessed a highly analytic mind. Her preparation for majoring in forensic science, however, was limited to a high school science course and a few semesters of introductory coursework in college. We began working together during her junior year, just after she joined a research laboratory.

Chapter Descriptions

The six students discussed in this book represent various ethnicities and socioeconomic classes. Each one also presented interesting insights into how underrepresented minorities develop rhetorical facility in scientific discourse. I have endeavored not simply to recount the intellectual work produced by each of these students but to explore the embodied experiences that emerged from our conversations. Because of this intent, there is an iterative aspect to the knowledge that was uncovered. The interrogation of White supremacy and patriarchy in STEM disciplines and in education occurs repeatedly throughout the text, with each iteration approaching the issue from a different angle. As a result, discussions of program structure and mentoring surface throughout. The goal is to illustrate the layering of oppression that occurred in these minoritized student experiences; like peeling an onion, each chapter focuses on one layer of impact, including strategies for mitigating harm.

In Chapter 1, I present the theoretical framework through which I examined these student experiences. In this interdisciplinary study, I draw on social psychology (e.g., Ahmed, 2006; Harré, 2004) to examine how students are positioned (by themselves and others) within institutional spaces based on visible and invisible markers (e.g., race/ethnicity, gender, class). I view this positioning through a lens of critical race theory and intersectionality (Crenshaw, 1991) to consider the ways various vectors of oppression impact students both systemically and interpersonally. Finally, I consider the ways in which counterspaces—physical and emotional spaces that disrupt oppression for marginalized groups—serve to disrupt harmful narratives about who belongs in STEM and who does not. This larger, interdisciplinary framework sets the foundation for examining White institutional presence ([WIP], Gusa, 2010) in practice.

Chapter 2 begins the data-based chapters, discussing WIP within the context of science and education broadly and the institution specifically. The focus is to demonstrate how WIP manifests in educational and disciplinary spaces and the impact this can have on students' development as academic and disciplinary writers. Despite being both an HSI and MSI, WIP was still a factor in students' experiences both at John Jay and in PRISM. This chapter includes insights into how the program design and mentors reinforced and pushed against systemic bias in STEM, and it also presents insights into the students' orientation to their disciplines (including awareness of discrimination).

Chapter 3 explores how race-evasive and culture-conscious ideologies influenced participants' interactions with scientific discourse. Drawing on Eduardo Bonilla-Silva's (2002) discussion of "color-blind" ideology, I examine the ways in which mentors and students considered race and gender in academic and disciplinary contexts. I also explore how positioning the scientific discourse as either normal and common or as a new language to be learned influenced whether or not students saw themselves as having a right (and an ability) to use the discourse in their present and future work. This chapter also discusses concerns of race and gender representation in various disciplinary spaces.

Chapter 4 begins with a discussion of speech acts, drawing heavily on James L. Austin (1975), John R. Searle (1969), and Rom Harré (2009), to explain how language creates and maintains institutional spaces. Included is an examination of how speech acts work in STEM education, with an emphasis on the physical sciences. The primary focus of the chapter, however, is to illustrate how language functions in STEM educational spaces to include or exclude students. Drawing on the experiences of the participants in this study, I show how speech acts can create an institutional space of inclusivity or further marginalize through microaggressions, marking individuals as members of the disciplinary community, or not.

Chapter 5 discusses the ways in which PRISM is physically and organizationally structured so as to create space for a counterspace to emerge. More than simply a safe space, a counterspace provides respite—a physical, mental, and emotional space where oppressions due to race/ethnicity, gender, and/or class can be challenged by those with a shared identity. As Micere Keels (2019) has noted, counterspaces are spaces that allow for radical growth—"the development of ideas and narratives that challenge dominant representations of and notions about . . . marginalized identities" (p. 2). Through an examination of narrative identity work, the ways in which people can read their disciplines as a unique culture, the accommodation of student needs in mentor-pairing, and the provision of space for resistance, the chapter outlines some of the ways programs can set a foundation for inclusion and accountability work.

In the final chapter, I extend the discussions of the case studies and factors that push students from or pull them toward disciplinary spaces to provide practical considerations for educators. This chapter explicitly focuses on applications that can be immediately enacted in educational spaces. The book concludes with suggestions of new areas for research.

Chapter 1. The Intersection of Language, Culture, and Power

We author "selves" whenever we speak or write—through the language choices we select, our intonation and rhythm, how we engage with genres, and how we read our audience. Roz Ivanič (1998) defines this process as the making of the "discoursal self"—the impression individuals create through discourse of who they are—noting, "Every time people write, they reaffirm or contest the patterns of privileging among subject positions which are sustained by the relations of power in the institution within which they are writing" (p. 33). This discoursal self is mediated by the "autobiographical self"—the writer's "sense of themselves" within these institutions and power relations (p. 33). As Sara Ahmed (2006) reminds us, however, our sense of self is also impacted by our "conditions of arrival" (p. 41). These conditions include the story of how we got here, the things we came in contact with, and the bits we picked up and that stuck to us along the way. She explains, "You bring your past encounters with you when you arrive" (p. 40). These encounters and experiences are laminated onto one another and, over time, become difficult (if not impossible) to separate from one another.

Like these encounters and experiences, the framework through which I examine the student experiences presented in this book is also laminated. I begin with five key premises that ground my understanding of students' sense of selves within institutional spaces:

1. As both Lev S. Vygotsky (1978) and Wenger (1998) have demonstrated, learning is a social activity. While people can learn in isolation, it is through interaction with others—observing the reception of our words and ideas and engaging in discourse—that we truly build mastery and understand areas for growth.

2. Mastery of content knowledge and discoursal skill are intertwined. As we understand concepts, so too do we begin to understand the terminology associated with those concepts. They become part of an individual's vocabulary and discourse options.

3. This learning of content knowledge and discoursal skill takes time but can be sped up or slowed down based on internal and external factors.

4. Becoming a member of a group—disciplinary or otherwise—is a process of negotiating our existing identity and determining whether the beliefs and values of the new group align or conflict with our existing identities and storylines. Language is intertwined with this group belonging.

5. How we are reflected back to ourselves via others plays a role in our felt experience and group belonging.

Laminated onto these premises are some additional key considerations. Keeping in mind the "stickiness" and heterogeneity Ahmed (2006) refers to, we need to remember some of the tenets of critical race theory offered by Gloria Ladson-Billings and William F. Tate (1995), as well as others (Bell, 1992; Crenshaw, 1991; Gillborn, 2006; Solorzano & Delgado Bernal, 2001; Solórzano & Yosso, 2002; Tate, 1997), so that we understand that the conditions of arrival for BIPOC STEM students are not the same as for their White counterparts:

- Race and racism are central fixtures of U.S. society. They are so endemic to our institutions that the way we do things *appears* neutral (Bonilla-Silva, 2018); race and racism are there, but in a way that we do not necessarily see them (Ahmed, 2006, p. 37).
- Race and racism intersect with other forms of oppression to the degree that it is nearly impossible to parse the negative impacts of one oppression from another, but these impacts compound when multiple vectors of oppression are present (Crenshaw, 1991).
- Meritocracy—the belief that anyone can pull themselves up from the bootstraps (Villanueva, 1993) and succeed through hard work and grit—is a pernicious, persistent myth because it ignores systemic barriers unequally distributed throughout U.S. society.
- Experiential knowledge (DeCuir-Gunby et al., 2019, p. 6) is central to understanding the lived experiences of historically marginalized people in STEM. We cannot know the felt experiences without *listening* to their stories (Collins, 2000). Ignoring such stories, or writing them off as outliers, causes harm.
- Unpacking epistemological understanding of race and racism must be part of the process of counteracting and dismantling oppression. Working across disciplinary spaces is part of understanding the "complexity and intricateness" of race and racism in practice (DeCuir-Gunby et al., 2019, p. 6).

Furthermore, while the conditions of arrival are not the same across racial categories, they also are also not the same across gender or class. Like racism, sexism and classism are endemic to U.S. systems. Myths of meritocracy also impact female and low-income students because they ignore the extra set of challenges that need to be surmounted to reach the baseline. Epistemological understandings of gender and poverty also need critical examination, particularly in disciplinary spaces. There is a monumental amount of work to be done to even approximate an equal playing field.

Throughout this book, I unpack how race and racism, gender and patriarchy, and class and classism are systematized into the epistemologies, discourses, and practices of STEM disciplines, and I relate the felt experiences of individuals as they negotiated these discoursal spaces. Student experiences show how, as a new discourse is acquired, existing identities can be called into question and allegiances can be challenged, even as the new discourse opens students up to new opportunities and communities. Further, the interplay of these factors work to either drive students from a space or attract them toward it—push and pull factors, respectively. Within the context of disciplinary and educational spaces, researchers can think of these push and pull factors as the factors that draw students toward a discipline and/or educational institution and as the factors that may cause them to feel pushed out or unwelcome. Within these disciplinary and educational spaces, push and pull factors should be viewed as often-subtle influences that convey to students their place—their position—within the space. These include, but are not limited to, the institutionalization of particular belief systems, teaching practices, and societal expectations that allow for structural patterns of inequity to persist within the US (Guess, 2006). Denying the presence of racism, sexism, and classism within these different spheres contributes to the perpetuation of hostility and discrimination (Gusa, 2010); explicitly addressing them in a way that creates spaces to subvert them can assist in the creation of welcoming, inclusive environments (Ong et al., 2018).

Developing discoursal skill as a member of a community should never be about assimilating into another's discourse; instead, it should be about negotiation and embodiment with agency—adopting some or all of it as one's own, which includes agency to critique and modify it. It should emphasize understanding one's self in light of the new discourse. Because language has

> the potential to conceal as well as disclose, any struggle over language at the same time entails a struggle over worlds fought on the deepest levels of the self—that part of the self that most intimately connects with other selves and with history. (Spellmeyer, 1998, p. 258)

To take on a new discourse as one's own requires recognizing that the discourse has the ability to describe an aspect of one's self that other discourses cannot adequately represent.

In the case studies presented in this text, I examine how various push factors influenced individual students as they attempted to learn the practices and discourse of science. Importantly, I also discuss the pull factors—practices and approaches that counteracted these negative messages—that helped students both see a place for themselves within the discipline as well as see the discourse of science as one that belonged to them. As Diane Lynn Gusa (2010) notes, when people "neglect to identify the ways in which White ideological homogenizing practices sustain the structure of domination and oppression, they allow institutional policies and practices to be seen as unproblematic or inevitable and thereby perpetuate hostile racial climates" (p. 465). When we know better, we are obligated to do better. This text will contribute to educators' and administrators' ability to do better.

Discourse and Identity

Bryan Brown and colleagues (2005) have argued that, given the "notion that all forms of discourse come to symbolize cultural membership and identity," those interested in science education particularly should be conscious of the complications that students face in "the literate practices of science" (p. 790). Knowledge, scientific or otherwise, is constructed by the individual in conjunction with others and can have powerful effects on student identity. As such, Brown and his coauthors suggest that educators should understand identity as a "resource as well as an artifact of classroom interaction. As students position themselves via discourse, they allow themselves to access specific knowledge and conceptual understanding that might otherwise be out of their reach" (p. 790). Discourse, in this sense, is more than a series of linguistic features and rhetorical moves. It serves as a gateway to other ways of knowing, seeing, and thinking that are socially constructed by the individuals circulating within specific discursive spaces.

At the same time, the individual's selection of which language to take up and how to take it up either reinforces or critiques the status quo. As Ivanič (1998) notes, using a specific discourse "is an act of identity in which people align themselves with socio-culturally shaped possibilities for self-hood, playing their part in reproducing or challenging dominant practices and discourses, and the values, beliefs and interests which they embody" (p. 32). The nature of these variations makes discourse inherently political; it is deeply embedded in struggles for power, is rooted in social structures, and is ideologically shaped (Fairclough, 1992, p. 17). How people see themselves, the world, and their places in the world impacts the ways they take up and engage in professional discourses.

In her conceptualizing of queer phenomenology, Ahmed (2006) has articulated how individuals orient themselves to certain possibilities and ways of knowing: "bodies," as well as identities, "take shape through tending toward objects that are reachable, that are available within the bodily horizon" (p. 2). Which objects, which opportunities, and which discourses are within people's spheres as they grow and mature? Which of these are not within any line of sight? The objects, people, opportunities, and discourses people come in contact with affect them in significant ways and orient them toward some things and away from others.

In the context of this research, what this means is that, as students entered PRISM, they were choosing to orient themselves toward STEM as a career, but their orientation markers—their points of entry and of understanding what this choice actually meant, what it looked and sounded like in practice—were quite different from one another and based on their prior exposures (through school, television, family, etc.). Those orientations to the discipline are discussed in the next chapter, but it is important to note here that as students entered the program, they were not very aware of the possibilities for self-hood within this new disciplinary sphere. Their orientation toward research and disciplinary discourse was rooted largely in laboratory work and readings related to coursework, with few exceptions. This orientation had its first immediate effect on mentor selection, but importantly it also impacted how students identified where they fit—how they were *positioned*—within larger hierarchical social structures of the program and discipline.

Wendy Holloway (1984) introduced the concept of "positioning" into the realm of social psychology and gender studies, using it as a means to conceptualize gender differences and subjectivity in discourse, arguing that

> discourses make available positions for subjects to take up. These positions are in relation to other people. Like the subject and object of a sentence . . . , women and men are placed in relation to each other through the meanings which a particular discourse makes available. (p. 236)

This conceptual framework allowed Holloway to make claims as to why women speak less frequently in mixed-gender groups than they do in gender-homogenous groups—her explanation being that in heterogeneous groups, women are positioned as having fewer rights than the male group members. Such positioning, Holloway argues, is something done to women and takes away a woman's ability to act. It is a social situation that is more *felt* than explicitly stated. Through life experiences, all individuals learn what they can get away with saying and doing in particular circumstances and what they cannot (often accompanied by a fear of reprisal or very real concerns for one's safety).

Positioning theory, as Holloway's (1984) concept has come to be known in the decades since, has become a foundation block of discursive psychology and has proven to be a useful tool for examining identity in practice. It is, as Harré (2004) explains, "the study of the way rights and duties are taken up and laid down, ascribed and appropriated, refused and defended in the fine grain of the encounters of daily lives" (p. 4). With each speech act (whether spoken or written), people locate themselves as well as others within larger communities and contexts and "ascribe rights and claim them for ourselves and place duties on others" (Moghaddam & Harré, 2010, pp. 2–3).

It is worth noting that the terms "rights" and "duties" are quite loaded. In positioning theory, becoming a group insider is not as simple as performing appropriately. At its heart is the examination of the rights and duties people believe they have within a given context, as well as those rights and duties others ascribe to them. What people do (and say/write) within a given situation is dictated both by what they are physically and cognitively able to do, as well as what they believe they are permitted or forbidden to do based on historically and culturally situated storylines (Bonilla-Silva, 2018, p. 97). Storylines are developed in response to the experiences and encounters individuals have had along their journeys to this moment, but they are also informed by the ways individuals are oriented. "How do we begin to know," Ahmed (2006) asks,

> or to feel where we are, or even where we are going, by lining our-
> selves up with the features of the grounds we inhabit, the sky that
> surrounds us, or the imaginary lines that cut through our maps?
> How do we know which way to turn to reach our destination? (p. 6)

As individuals navigate new spaces, learning the lay of the land as they go, they are developing new reference points and inferring the social contracts at play in the space. In turning toward one possibility, they are turning their back on another, and that orientation is impacted by the things that have stuck to them along the way. Such things include an individual's personal history (what they have done or been perceived as in the past, including group histories like race, gender, class, and educational experience) as well as their individual attributes (i.e., mental, character, moral). For example, the storylines that women are too sensitive and not critical enough to do science or that individuals of Asian descent are natu-rally adept at mathematics have direct implications for how these individuals are perceived—and perceive themselves—in STEM educational settings. Such beliefs (which include stereotypes) can directly or indirectly position someone favorably or unfavorably within a given context.

"Positions," Rom Harré and Fathali Moghaddam (2003) argue, "exist as pat-terns of beliefs in the members of a relatively coherent speech community," which are reified in discourse conventions, performativity, and epistemology (p. 4). For example, within discussions of biological processes, we frequently see terms like "maleness" used to refer to organisms that provide something in a reproductive process (e.g., a fertility factor in bacteria), while those organisms without said factor are referred to as "female." Though seemingly innocuous, designations like this reinforce the idea of females being helpless and lacking and the idea that males are the provider and supporter in critical processes—even when discussing organisms, such as bacteria, that do not possess sexual organs. When discussing race, science textbooks often explore the topic from a seemingly impartial view-point that nevertheless embraces a particular belief system about the relationship between genetics and race. As Ann Morning (2008) illustrates in her systematic review of science textbooks from 1952 through 2002, contemporary textbooks often approach race through taxonomic and genetic lenses under the guise of inherited medical disorders. As she put it, the "overall impact of genetics has been to bolster, rather than challenge [essentialist views on race]," leaving an impres-sion that, in addition to phenotypic differences across racial categories, that there are also differences connected to competencies (i.e., intellect)—a clear connec-tion to the eugenics movements of the 19th and early 20th centuries (p. 125).

However, positioning goes much deeper than simply adhering to discourse conventions. Bronwyn Davies and Rom Harré (1990) took up Henri Tajfel and John Turner's (1979) model of social identity theory, arguing that how we see and interpret ourselves, the world, and our place in the world involves a series of interconnected processes. We must first understand that categories exist that include some individuals while excluding others (for example, gender, race, and socioeconomic class). We must also participate in discursive practices through which these categories are not only reinforced but also ascribed meaning (e.g., White is good, girls are sensitive). Then, we must position ourselves in relation to these categories and meanings, which "involves imaginatively positioning oneself as if one belongs in one category and not in the other" (Davies & Harré, 1990, p. 49). This imaginative positioning involves being oriented in specific ways—recognizing oneself as having the attributes and characteristics of a group and subsequently committing to the group and "the development of a moral system organized around the belonging" (p. 49). This moral system is deeply tied to the ways of being in the group—what it means to perform as a member of the group (for example, scientists have a moral obligation to be objective and conduct methodologically sound research). The degree to which individuals adhere to—assimilate into—this moral system is intricately linked to their perception by others (their positioning by others) as group insiders.

James Paul Gee (2000) notes that an individual is recognized as a "certain 'kind of person'" whenever they act or interact with others, and that the "kind of person" they are recognized as is mediated by the interaction's context and participants (p. 99). This "certain 'kind of person' in a given context" is what Gee means—and in this text, what I mean—by "identity" (p. 99). Since there are a multitude of interactions individuals can participate in, "all people have multiple identities," multiple selves, based on how they perform—or position themselves—in a given interaction or space (p. 99). As Harré and Moghaddam (2003) have explained, "people can adopt, strive to locate themselves in, be pushed into, be displaced from or be refused access . . . [to groups] in a highly mobile and dynamic way" (p. 6). This last facet becomes salient when considering work with marginalized groups in science where a lack of representation for women and BIPOC plays an important role in the socially constructed categorization of "scientist." It is through these lenses that we can begin to understand the systemic ways various vectors of oppression can operate in society and groups.

Positionality and Intersecting Vectors of Oppressions

A critical first step of orienting toward a disciplinary space and identity relies on recognizing that such possibilities exist for oneself to begin with. It is only when we see that these possibilities are within our social spheres that we can move toward them with an eye toward belonging. But, as explained in the previous section, how we position ourselves within the hierarchies is impacted by the rights and duties we see as being internally and externally ascribed to us: what are we allowed to do and not allowed to do within this space?

Because of these rights and duties, positioning is not the sole domain of one's own perceptions. It is not incumbent on individuals alone to decide that they can claim a space and belong within a discipline. The "you can be anything if you believe in yourself" perspective ignores that there are very real vectors of oppression working to reinforce and reinscribe particular social structures and hierarchies. As Rebecca Walton and colleagues (2019) have argued effectively, power within a space is directly correlated with positionality and privilege. How we are oriented and the space we see ourselves as being able occupy are directly implicated by who we are in relation to others, what our identities mean, historically, within a given space at a specific moment in time, individual conceptualization about what it means to occupy particular roles, and how our identities interact with normative conceptions of a specific role. Because of this, we cannot talk about disciplinarity, identity, and social categorizations like race, gender, and class, without explicitly addressing intersectionality.

This often-misused term does *not* refer to the multiple identities an individual may possess (e.g., "my intersectional identities"); rather, it explicitly refers to the vectors of oppression an individual experiences as a *result* of their multiple identities. In the United States, BIPOC individuals experience oppressions related to race that White individuals do not, and women experience oppressions that men do not. Female BIPOC individuals experience *compounding* and sometimes distinct oppressions of both race and gender.

In her seminal work on intersectionality, legal scholar Kimberlé Crenshaw (1989) offers a frame through which to see these multiple vectors of oppression operating on individuals. As she explains early in the piece, when considering the law,

> in race discrimination cases, discrimination tends to be viewed in terms of sex- or class-privileged Blacks; in sex discrimination cases, the focus is on race- and class-privileged women. This focus on the most privileged group members marginalizes those who are multiply-burdened and obscures claims that cannot be understood as resulting from discrete sources of discrimination. (p. 140)

In STEM equity research, the ignoring of intersectionality plays out regularly: the overwhelming majority of research on gender has focused on the experiences of White women, and the overwhelming majority of research on race/ethnicity has focused on males. Disturbingly little research has been conducted with individuals who not only have the double oppression of being both female and a racial/ethnic minority but also the third oppression of their chosen discipline— science (Cobb, 1976; Ong et al., 2011). The examination of intersectional identities of BIPOC women within science disciplines is necessary if we as a nation are truly interested in increasing the number of women and minorities not simply studying but also *working* in STEM disciplines. It is also critical in this research to ask whether the focus on men of color and White women in STEM has had the unintentional consequence of once again "othering" minority women by reinforcing a stereotype that BIPOC women do not exist in STEM disciplines and/or are not interested in pursuing STEM careers.[4] Without critically examining the conditions of schooling for minority women, we may be unintentionally excluding and also obscuring areas ripe for reform.

A Case for Counterspaces

In the preceding sections, I have laid out the interdisciplinary approach I take in this book toward thinking about the experiences of my research participants and their discoursal skill development as they engaged in undergraduate research in STEM. By considering how humans orient themselves to new spaces, how they are positioned as individuals *within* those spaces, and how their identities inform how they see themselves in these spaces (as well as how others see them), researchers can then begin to unpack the ways in which these forces impact discursive practices.

For the students in this study White institutional presence (WIP; discussed in detail in the next chapter) played a role in their engagement with scientific discourse and the scientific community despite the college being recognized as a Hispanic- and Minority-serving institution and despite targeted efforts to improve retention and persistence. WIP is embedded within STEM disciplines and education broadly. Understanding the profession, leadership roles, and networking behaviors presented one level of barrier to students attempting to engage with the authentic work of undergraduate research. A lack of career models, stereotyping, narratives of grit, and ascription of intelligence presented another level. Combined with language associations, concerns about tokenism, and insecurity regarding self-sufficiency, these barriers impacted students' early engagement with both scientific discourse and the community.

As will become evident in the telling of these students' stories, there is a need for marginalized individuals in STEM disciplines (and other restricted disciplines) to have a space to breathe, push back, and form responses to outside oppressions (Collins, 2000; hooks, 1990; Smith, 2000). In 1991, Henri Lefebvre wrote that space

> shows itself to be *politically instrumental* in that it facilitates the control of society, while at the same time being a *means of production* by virtue of the way it is developed . . . ; underpins the reproduction of production relations and property relations (i.e., ownership of land, of space; hierarchical ordering of locations; organization of networks as a function of capitalism;

---

4. By way of example, while reviewing data collected by agencies such as the National Science Foundation, I observed that data are collected by race and gender but are not parsed by both (we know how many men and women are studying and working in STEM, but we do not know *exactly* how many of those women are women of color). This omission alone makes women of color in science invisible.

class structures; practical requirements); is equivalent, practically speaking, to a set of institutional and ideological superstructures that are not presented for what they are . . . ; and contains possibilities—of works and reappropriation—existing to begin within the artistic sphere but responding above all to the demands of a body "transported" outside of itself in space, a body which by putting up resistance inaugurates the project of a different space (either the space of a counter-culture, or a counter-space in the sense of an initially utopian alternative to actually existing in "real" space). (p. 349)

In other words, space is not apolitical—spaces "are made for some kinds of bodies more than others" (Ahmed, 2006, p. 51). Spaces position individuals through hierarchies, systematize bias in ways that are invisible, and reify particular ways of being and knowing (which I illustrate at the beginning of the next chapter). Critically, they also hold the potential for disruption through counterspaces. Counterspaces are a place to actualize resistance to the status quo. They provide a space to create a reality that does not reinscribe traditional rights and duties and allows for the *turning toward* potential futures described by Ahmed (2006) without necessarily turning *against* culture or history.

Though Lefebvre (1991) did not fully define the concept of counterspaces, nor did he offer insight into their construction or maintenance, others have taken up this concept and filled these gaps. For example, Daniel Solórzano and his colleagues (2000) describe such spaces in education as "sites where deficit notions of people of color can be challenged and where a positive collegiate racial climate can be established and maintained" (p. 70). Counterspaces are intentional spaces where individuals with a shared identity can be free to work, talk, study, etc., without the physical or emotional pressures of specific oppressions and without the presence of potential oppressors. For example, a group for women in engineering or a Black caucus within a national organization can serve as counterspaces. Such spaces can be created through organizations and affinity groups (e.g., fraternities and sororities) as well as between faculty and students who share particular characteristics (such as race, gender, disability, or sexual orientation).

Andrew D. Case and Carla D. Hunter (2012) further argue that counterspaces can and should be thought of as specific, intentional settings—spaces where individuals can develop positive self-concepts that challenge "deficit-oriented dominant cultural narratives and representations concerning these individuals" (p. 261). These settings play critical roles in enabling marginalized individuals to push against dominant narratives of exclusion or inadequacy through what the authors refer to as "adaptive responding" (p. 259). "Adaptive responding," they explain, "is the multidimensional psychosocial process occurring at the individual and setting level, which facilitates, in marginalized individuals, the capacity to circumvent, resist, counteract and/or mitigate the psychological experience of oppression" (p. 259). The mechanisms for which this process is actualized are, as noted above, multidimensional and include such things as self-protection, which may include using basic coping skills, avoidance, or confrontation, as well as the enhancement of self-concept. This latter mechanism may be enacted through narrative identity work (e.g., resisting traditional storylines related to race, gender, or discipline), acts of resistance (challenging traditional norms, etc.), and direct relational transactions (the relationships between individuals that foster agency and self-efficacy).

Much of the research on counterspaces has focused on predominantly White institutions (PWIs) where race is salient (Keels, 2019; Ong et al., 2018). In this book, I explore how counterspaces work within the confines of Hispanic- and Minority-serving institutions (HSIs and MSIs) where the dominant groups are not White (though the disciplinary and academic discourses are). Using Case and Hunter's (2012) framework, I explore how narrative identity work, acts of resistance, and direct relational transactions were enacted within PRISM as an institutional structure as well as explore interpersonal interactions that took place as part of the undergraduate research experience. While I go into specific detail in Chapters 5 and 6 about how these mechanisms are actualized in PRISM, throughout all of the chapters I discuss the ways in which student participants adopted or resisted traditional storylines of scientific identity, challenged norms, and built empowering relationships. Importantly, I also discuss the ways in which the program and individual mentors facilitated the development of a counterspace—even if it did not seem accessible to all students in PRISM. These findings lead to guidelines instructors, mentors, and programs can adopt to build inclusive spaces for BIPOC, women, and other minoritized individuals within STEM.

Chapter 2. Lifting the Curtain: Working With, and Against, White Institutional Presence in Science

In Chapter 1, I presented a framework for—my orientation to—how I am presenting and analyzing the student experiences in this book. In this chapter, I offer an explication of how White Institutional Presence manifests in STEM disciplinary and educational spaces. I follow this explication with a discussion of mentor understandings of how (if at all) these factors materialize in their work, student orientations to the field, and considerations and applications for this knowledge. This chapter sets the stage for a more detailed look at mentor-student interactions in Chapters 3 and 4 and the impacts on student writing and scientific identity.

A key tenet of critical race theory is that race and racism are central fixtures of U.S. society. They are so endemic to U.S. institutions that they become nearly invisible in everyday practice, creating "institutional and ideological superstructures that are not presented for what they [really] are" (Lefebvre, 1991, p. 349). Bonilla-Silva (2018) notes that racism itself is a "a network of social relations at the social, political, economic, and ideological levels that shapes the life chances of the various races" (p. 18). In order to understand this institutionalized structure, however, we have to begin by acknowledging the White Institutional Presence (WIP) that is pervasive and how it creates space to mask inequity. In her 2010 concept paper on WIP, Gusa examines how White cultural ideology is embedded "in the cultural practices, traditions, and perceptions of knowledge that are taken for granted as the norm of institutions of higher education" (p. 464). Whose histories are taught (Ruiz, 2016)? Whose languages and grammars are enforced (Baker-Bell, 2020; Inoue, 2019)? Whose ways of behaving in spaces are sanctioned? Whose methods of creating knowledge are accepted (Baber, 2019; Collins, 2000)?

Though there are multiple facets to WIP, one of the most insidious is White ascendancy, "the belief that one's ideas, knowledge, values, societal roles and norms, and understanding of history are universally and exclusively correct" (Gusa, 2010, p. 472). To be successful as a member of a given field, one must conform to the dominant ways of thinking, being, and doing. It is "the expectation that all individuals conform to one 'scholarly' worldview;" a worldview that is normed on those who have historically been in positions of power and domination (Gusa, 2010, p. 475) and leaves very little room for a multiplicity of viewpoints or historical experience. In education, and specifically science education, these beliefs, knowledge, and roles are normed according to White, male, middle-to-upper-class values because, historically, that is who has been allowed to participate in these spaces (Kachchaf et al,, 2015; Ong, 2005;)—what P. L. Thomas (2017) refers to as the "white male template" (para. 17).

Though an emphasis on objectivity and the scientific method may lead some to view science as arhetorical and acultural, in reality such an epistemology is a reflection of White ascendancy in practice. Biases are present in the social structures and daily routines of scientific fields: the understanding of scientific professions, their career models, and the effects of tokenism (Bird, 2011; Britton, 2010; Haas et al., 2016;); networking behaviors and professional selection processes, particularly in leadership roles (Hansen et al., 2019; van den Brink & Benschop, 2014;); and the stereotyping and disparaging of women and female qualities (Faulkner, 2007, 2008; Gilbert, 2009;). As Ann E. Cudd (2001) has argued in her ethno-feminist critique of the sciences, in order for science "to be objective with respect to its race and gender biases, it will need to constantly challenge those biases by bringing in scientists from race and gender minorities" (p. 81). This argument needs to be extended beyond representation, however, to include alternative ways of knowing and constructing knowledge (see Baber, 2019, for an excellent discussion of this).

Sexism, racism, and other forms of discrimination can be difficult to identify and change once they have become institutionalized; they become ingrained into everyday practices, as well as a part of assumptions that are unstated and unrecognized. As Cudd (2001) explains,

> Androcentrism infects a scientific theory when the theory assumes that the experiences, biology, and social roles of males or men are the norm and that of females or women is a deviation from the norm. Ethnocentrism infects a scientific theory when it assumes that the experiences, biologically based or socially created physical attributes or medical problems, and social roles of people of a particular ethnic or racial background are the norm and those with other backgrounds are deviations from the norm. (p. 86)

This homogenizing based on White and male experiences and values by default 'others' BIPOC and women by seeing them as an exception to the rule. These biases show themselves in science as epistemic values, argued by Ernan McMullin (1982) to be values "we have reason to believe will, if pursued, help toward the attainment of . . . knowledge" (p. 18). These values include, for example, the belief that simplicity is best in research design or the valuing of quantifiable data over qualitative. Biases also present as non-epistemic values (i.e., deciding which research projects to pursue or fund or identifying practical limitations of methodologies) (Diekmann & Peterson, 2013). Furthermore, not including sex or racial differences in parsing research data in study design and analysis, for example, "creates a situation where guidelines based on the study of one sex [or race] may be generalized and applied to both" (Holdcroft, 2007, p. 2).

Just as Crenshaw (1989) argues that an intersectional approach is necessary in legal spaces to account for compounding impacts of multiple vectors of oppression, so too is it necessary in STEM spaces. For example, research into coronary heart disease, autism, and stroke has predominantly focused on males, despite the knowledge that symptoms of each present very differently in females (Keville, 1994; Lee et al., 2017). Biomedical research studies on environmentally related diseases (e.g., asthma, cancer, diabetes) are less likely to include people of color in their participant cohorts than White counterparts, despite the reality that BIPOC communities are disproportionately affected by such health issues (Burchard et al., 2015; Konkel, 2015; Oh et al., 2015;). In fact, though Black and Latinx individuals make up over 30 percent of the U.S. population, they account for only six percent of the population in federally-funded clinical research trials (Oh, et al., 2015). Thus, we can see from a focus on research interest alone—what is funded and what is investigated—that there are important representational gaps.

Importantly, such value biases extend to the ways individuals and institutions decide how scientific knowledge is communicated and circulated in social spheres. Cherice Escobar Jones and Genesis Barco Medina (2021), for example, used corpus linguistic methods to analyze the conflation of race and biology in medical texts produced by the National Institutes of Health, highlighting the persistence of this conflation despite genomic understanding that race and biology do not correlate. These "bio-racial rhetorics" (as they have named the practice) perpetuate historical myths that there are biological differences between racial groups. Layer onto this a history of objectification, experimentation, and negation (e.g., the Tuskegee Syphilis Study and forced sterilization; Brandt, 1978; Ramírez, 2017), as well as misinformation campaigns, and it becomes apparent how science (and medicine, particularly) have been structured to privilege White, male, heterosexual bodies and diseases as the norm, and all others as outliers.

One need not look any further than the messaging surrounding SARS-CoV-2, the virus that causes COVID-19, and race/ethnicity to see not only the pseudo-scientific information circulated in the public sphere but also the consequences of the resulting distrust (Kreps & Kriner, 2020). In the early stages of the pandemic, for example, rumors circulated on Twitter and in major cities like Chicago and Atlanta that Black people were immune to COVID-19 (Armstrong, 2020). Conflicting information from scientists about mask-wearing and ways to contract the virus exacerbated doubt in many Americans and disproportionately impacted BIPOC communities, as they represent a significant portion of workers deemed "essential" and as such were placed in situations that put them at higher risk for contracting the virus. Throughout the first two years of the pandemic, Black Americans consistently had a COVID-19 mortality rate that was more than twice that of White Americans (Gawthrop, 2022). Combined with predominantly White faces providing the messaging from the scientific community, the result has been both a skepticism of science by communities of color as well as a perception that individuals from these groups do not do science.

In addition to social messages pushing faux science, individuals who pursue scientific fields are also exposed to academic microaggressions in the form of educator and institutional ideologies (discussed in Chapter 3). Such microaggressions present themselves in campus and disciplinary climates (in the form of who is visible, "color-blindness," how racial or gender bias-incidents are handled, etc.), instructional methods and the presentation of knowledge (including the pathologizing of cultural values and communication styles), and instructor beliefs (such as ascription of intelligence, myths of meritocracy) (Cooper et al., 2011). Any and all of these factors can push newcomers away from a discipline or institution. As Keels (2019) has explained, the

> prototypical student is White, male, middle or upper class, and has been validated in educational institutions and in broader societal representations through his life. In sharp contrast, many historically marginalized students come to college with a lifetime of negative interactions with those in positions of power in educational spaces. Those experiences are not erased upon entering college. (p. 16)

In education, WIP is manifested in policies and procedures that take into consideration the needs and resources of the prototypical student and that treat all others as outliers in need of remediation. It also plays out in the moment-by-moment interactions students have with peers and mentors. For example, for first-generation college students, the newness of college and the often-invisible academic expectations can be difficult to negotiate without the aid of a parent or mentor who can serve as a guide. As Keels (2019) noted in her case studies of women of color at a predominantly White university, something as simple as having an adult confirm the difficulty of college work for all students—to advise students to stick with it and not drop out—can play an important role in student success. Similarly, for many students from low socioeconomic communities, the lack of a rigorous high school curriculum or strategies for success can negatively impact their experiences engaging with college coursework. Instructors and peers who do not recognize such differences can unconsciously create environments that reinforce inequitable belief systems where microaggressions exist and where racial or gender performativity becomes an issue.

While I focus on mentor ideology explicitly in Chapter 3, it seems pertinent to take some time here to provide insight into how PRISM mentors conceptualized the culture of the scientific community broadly and the ways in which these practices and policies reified and responded to systemic bias. Doing so helps clarify how students and mentors were oriented to their fields and provides insight into the ways in which systemic bias seeped into the spaces explicitly meant to create access.

PRISM's Response to Inequity

PRISM was created in direct response to the inequity faculty members were seeing on the John Jay campus. There were clear demarcations in attrition based on racial demographics, and it was apparent that students from low socioeconomic backgrounds and BIPOC communities did not have access to the resources needed to participate in non-funded internships or externship opportunities outside of the college. Opportunities for undergraduate research that are common at R1 institutions were outside of the realm of possibility before this program was created.

Until the late 1990s, the institution offered its undergraduate students the opportunity to learn laboratory skills within the confines of specific courses and an external internship only. The support system for undergraduate research was lacking, active mentorship between the faculty and students was rare, and students were exposed minimally if at all to basic scientific research (Carpi, et al., 2013a). As the struggle to retain students in the science major became more and more apparent, so also did the expectations and aspirations of students who were successful academically. The proportion of students pursuing graduate school was miniscule; most saw the program as vocational training and considered their next logical step to be an entry-level job placement as a technician in a crime laboratory. Junior and senior forensics students were failing to see themselves as scientists or capable of getting post-graduate degrees, and many could not see where such degrees could lead them. As a result, a small group of faculty within the Department of Sciences recognized the potential to create opportunities that would increase student understanding of what it means to have a career in the sciences, feel part of the academic and scientific community, and actively engage with the scientific process. It was believed that, by increasing opportunities for mentorship and social connections as well as by building an academic support framework, upper-level students would be more engaged and the institution would see higher incidences of academic success in STEM, including an increase in women and BIPOC students going on to post-graduate programs leading to high-level careers.

As noted in the Introduction to this book, the pedagogical goals in creating the program were three-fold: (a) to facilitate the engagement of students with the forensic science curriculum so as to assist their passage through the major; (b) to increase graduate/professional school acceptance rates and career success for graduates; and (c) to assist in the creation of a professional community that would extend beyond their years at the institution (Carpi et al., 2013a). These goals in-and-of-themselves are laudable. What was not taken into consideration at the time, however, was the systematic, institutionalized racism and sexism that exists in the STEM disciplines as a whole. It was assumed that teaching women and BIPOC students how to conduct research would be enough to increase their presence in the various STEM disciplines the college offers. The onus of discrimination in STEM was placed on individual practitioners—an occasional bad actor—and not the system as a whole. Though there was no conscious attempt to do so, what was enacted was more a program of assimilation than one of acculturation. It would fall on individual mentors to enact the program in more equitable and inclusive ways.

In my interviews with mentors, when they discussed the culture of science broadly, there was enough consistency across program mentors to conclude that they generally saw STEM as being meritocratic. One mentor explained that the only way to develop "street cred" was through publishing papers. For example, when discussing molecular biology, this mentor explained that

> it's a discipline that is much more meritorious than society in general. If you're from a crappy school or crappy, even, country, that doesn't necessarily hurt you. It's the quality of your work. Every once in a while, you'll see a paper in the biggest journals from countries you've never heard of, even, that discovered something really cool and they were really, truly given a shot.

From this quotation alone, it is evident that some WIP persists. While people can recognize that "crappy schools" (meaning, underfunded) exist throughout the US, what exactly is a "crappy country"? If somebody from such a place—somebody from a country we have "never heard of"—is able to publish in a top journal, does that mean that the process is meritocratic? Or, does it mean that that author managed to overcome barriers and find a way through? Though this mentor felt that the system was "not perfect," they also felt that "it's better than society as a whole in terms of how you earn respect." The unconscious assumption this mentor made was that following the rules of how science is done is enough, mirroring scientific ontology that anyone should be able to conduct a procedure and acquire the same, or similar, results *as long as they follow the rules*. But little consideration is given to who makes these rules, how explicit they are to newcomers, or how easy they are to enact.

While all mentors described the culture in ways that emphasized grit (e.g., "you have to pay your dues"), a few drew attention to the ways in which STEM disciplines, broadly, are linguistically biased. To be taken seriously as a member of a STEM discipline, one not only needs to communicate in English ("English is the language of science right now") but also needs to use English in a way that conforms to the "cold, dry style" that is "very matter-of-fact and heavily passive voice." Only one mentor that participated in this study ever claimed a right to "write against the grain"—to push language expectations in scientific articles. Notably, this was a White, male scholar who also wrote for popular audiences. When asked if they also did this, all of the female and BIPOC mentors emphatically said "no"—that was not something they risked.

In a discussion of linguistic bias in STEM fields, Miguel Clavero (2011) argued that scholars who are non-native English speakers "support all the costs of having a [sic] English as a common scientific language" (p. 156). In addition to the extra labor required to learn English fluently enough to communicate complicated scientific concepts, non-native English speaking scientists also are confronted with linguistic difficulties as they relate to publication bias. There are strong correlations between scholars' first language and their publication productivity (see, for example, Man et al., 2004; Primack et al., 2009; Vasconcelos et al., 2008). Similarly, discrepancies in publication rates between women and men continue to be marked. Marc J. Lerchenmueller and Olav Sorenson (2018) found that, in the life sciences specifically, women become principal investigators on grants at a rate 20 percent slower than men, with publication rates and citation practices playing critical roles in the lag. While the roots of these discrepancies are different, both impacted mentors' willingness to take chances in writing because their identities marked them as other.

Despite linguistic bias in the field, though, it was quite common to hear mentors and mentees in PRISM conversing in a variety of languages and dialects (predominantly Spanish and African American Vernacular English). Program and promotional materials, as well as other outward-facing documents, were also frequently offered in both English and Spanish, normalizing PRISM (and by extension STEM) as multilingual. Notably, two PRISM mentors who were *not* part of this study ran a "Minority Women in STEM" program at the college to help break down barriers around gender and identity, as well. None of the students in this research participated, however, as this program was focused on graduate students at the time.

Because "publication is our currency" in STEM disciplines (as one mentor put it), these linguistic and gender differences would seem critical to highlight when teaching and training underrepresented minorities in these fields. Yet, they were rarely, if ever, discussed when it related to writing. Rather, the unarticulated assumptions were that students would need to work extra hard to overcome these biases, not that the biases themselves needed addressing.

Where the program and faculty mentors *did* seem aware of inequity was in regard to access to career models and understanding disciplinary networking behaviors. As part of the PRISM programming, individuals from a wide variety of relevant STEM fields are frequently invited to give guest lectures on their research. Open to all members of the college's STEM community, these guest speakers are intentionally drawn from a wide variety of career sectors to illustrate the many options available to students after graduation. Importantly, these individuals also typically represent marginalized communities in STEM. In this way, students are regularly exposed to people who look and sound like them in positions of power and who can illustrate paths to successful careers.

Similarly, efforts are made regularly to help students acculturate into the ways of participating in and performing at disciplinary conferences, a key locale for professional networking. These efforts are supported at two distinct levels. The first is through an annual symposium that asks students to create and present scientific posters explaining their research (this symposium will be discussed in greater detail later in the book). Through workshops on how to create such posters and strategies for speaking to an audience of varying expertise, students are prepared for their first encounters with academic conferences and often report feeling an increased sense of autonomy and pride with regard to their undergraduate research work. The second, more advanced level of professional networking occurs through preparing students to apply to, attend, and present at regional and national conferences. Through assistance in the preparation of abstracts and presentations as well as instruction in how to apply for conference funding to cover travel and attendance fees, students are encouraged to present their research beyond the immediate college community. In these experiences, mentors also assist students in networking behaviors typical of the field: teaching students how to make introductions and small talk, helping students connect with other scholars, and assisting them in navigating new professional spaces. By providing access to these ways of communicating and performing in a transparent way, students gain access to critical information that contributes to career success: making connections, becoming known, and sharing scholarship with disciplinary experts for immediate feedback. These conference experiences not only can lead to graduate school opportunities and professional positions after graduating, but also provide students an opportunity to peek behind the curtain of how professionals in their field present new scholarship and work on new ideas. Through this exposure, students have opportunities to reevaluate how they are oriented to their fields as well as reconsider their places within them.

By examining program and mentor orientations to their fields, it becomes clear that even in programs designed to increase access and even at institutions that are designated as HSIs and MSIs, systemic bias can remain invisible in important ways. While representation and opportunities to conduct research are important, those efforts can be unraveled if the epistemologies grounding them are not also examined. Understanding the hidden barriers in spaces students are entering becomes a critical part of also understanding the dynamics that unfold as they negotiate their identities and reorient themselves as undergraduate researchers.

Students' Understanding of the Profession: Why Science?

Like their mentors, students were also oriented toward STEM disciplines in particular ways that impacted their development and growth as members of the disciplinary community. Why did they choose science as a career and were they aware of discrepancies within STEM disciplines in terms of racial and gender makeup? These are particularly salient questions for individuals who are largely underrepresented in their fields and do not have immediate role models.

Ruben, a single father who also worked 30 hours a week on a construction site, was very intentional about his decision to pursue science as a career. He began his academic career at one of the partnering community colleges and then transferred to John Jay after two years. When I first asked him why he chose science over other majors available, he was enthusiastic and proud of his choice, saying,

> I think science can benefit society and also can benefit me,
> because I think science is important. It's invaluable. And I think
> that's what I [want] . . . to be better and be important. Not as a
> selfish [sic] or as pride. I just want to be useful.

This altruism was not without its complications, though. Ruben was well aware of the academic challenges that were ahead of him:

> I was afraid at the beginning. I was afraid of math and science
> at the advanced level, but I realized that I'm sacrificing my time
> to be in college, so I'd rather do something that is more valuable
> than just . . . I mean other majors are *valuable*, but I just thought
> science will open more doors, more jobs, and that's what . . .
> how I came to a decision to study science.

In addition to being the first person in his family to attend college, Ruben did not have any role models in his personal life who demonstrated for him what a scientific life might look like. Like many students in my study, his exposure to science came largely from television programs and marketing materials circulating in high schools and in the public sphere. As he articulated in our first conversation, pursuing a career in science was as much about mobilizing up the socioeconomic ladder toward security as it was about contributing to the world.

When asked specifically if race ever factored into his thoughts about his career, he responded matter-of-factly: "No, I don't think about race. I mean, I know sometimes it might have an effect. It might have an effect on getting a job or whatever, maybe. But I don't . . . I feel confident enough." Ruben felt strongly that, though there may be discrimination in other parts of the US, this was not an issue in New York City because of its racial and economic diversity. His plan was to complete his bachelor's degree, follow up with a master's degree, then secure a good job.

Ruben was not alone in believing in a narrative of grit. Anne, who identified as a Black cis-female, had come to the college to study forensic science after being inspired by female scientists in television shows like *CSI* and *Dr. G Medical Examiner*. With the goal of becoming a medical examiner, Anne demonstrated a zest for life and learning from the moment we first spoke, noting, "My mom tells me all the time that there's not enough *me* to go around and do all of the stuff that I want to do." Though she was enthusiastic about pursuing this degree and what it might mean in terms of contributing to the world, Anne had absorbed some of her mother's concerns that she might not be ready for the academic work, a doubt that persisted even after her success in coursework. This doubt largely was based in not understanding the expectations that she would face in college. As a result, Anne approached each step cautiously. "I usually just take it one step at a time," she explained; "I feel like every level in life I say that the work can't get any harder than what it is, 'til I actually move up another level and be like [*in a soft voice*] 'Oh my God, it just got harder!'"

Though she claimed to be relatively unfocused prior to college—her professional interests ranged from modeling to photography, ballerina to veterinarian—Anne was committed enough in her schooling to not only attend the top high school in her district but also concentrate her academics on science. Anne's schooling was based on the British system, where students take all subjects for the first three years, then begin to "stream" according to career desires and aptitude. She earned her "O-levels"[5] in biology, chemistry, and physics. Rather than continue into the more advanced "A-levels," which are prerequisites for attending a university in the British system, Anne chose to leave school at 16 and move to the United States with her mother. Because of the differences in the schooling systems, Anne's mother wanted her to repeat high school in the US, but Anne resisted, agreeing only to "redo it" if she was not accepted into college. Her acceptance into John Jay ensured that she would not need to "backtrack." It also ensured an affordable education. Two of the key reasons she attended the college, rather than other schools that offered similar degrees, were because it was "cheaper" and because the proximity to home meant that she would have family supports. "I really can't support myself," she joked, "and I can't cook. So I need to stay home—or somewhere close to home—because I need to eat."

Like Ruben, Anne was unconcerned about discrimination in scientific fields at the start of the study, though she was aware of differences in terms of gender and racial representation:

> I mean, from what I see, I think it's mostly Caucasian people. Maybe I'm not looking hard enough. I could be wrong. But what I have observed so far, I've never seen a Black teacher [in science outside of John Jay]. So maybe this is not because of race, but I feel like Caucasian people are more fortunate, they tend to pay for med. school easier than if . . . for a person who's my color. And then people who are my color are not really that smart. We might be smart, but we tend to be stupid, as well. I don't know if you know what I'm getting at. Like, they make wrong decisions.

As Anne continued to talk, it became clear that the "wrong decisions" she was referring to had more to do with Black people's understanding and accepting the cultural negotiations of academia than they did with inherent intelligence (a conflation of race with socioeconomics). These decisions had to do with their ability to successfully navigate a system that was not familiar and with less preparation than their White, middle-class peers. Some of these so-called poor choices involved things like choosing a different career path because of fear, difficulty, or prejudice, as well as not being willing to adopt the ways in which particular fields operate. Like Ruben, Anne felt discrimination was a nonissue at John Jay because of its diverse student

---

5.   O-levels in the British system are the equivalent of general requirements to graduate high school in the United States. A-levels are on par with Advanced Placement coursework, though slightly more rigorous.

and faculty body as well as its location in New York City. To Anne, gender and race were not an issue because everyone was already so different from one another.

While Natalia and Amrita had similar reasons for pursuing degrees in science (i.e., contributing to society and mobilizing upward economically), their understanding of inequity in the larger disciplinary community was different. As Amrita, an Indian American woman, explained, the diversity of the college created a space where discrimination was not an obvious issue, but it seemed like an issue elsewhere:

> I think it's lucky that we're in a school like John Jay. I think John Jay probably has one of the most diverse [groups of] professors. I think it actually becomes an issue when students are *applying* to outside graduate programs or—I don't know about jobs, but graduate programs are . . . From what I hear, it's rare for a student from John Jay to be accepted at Harvard, Yale, or you know one of *those* colleges.

Natalia, a first-generation Latinx woman, similarly approached her collegiate experience with eyes wide open. In addition to providing important content knowledge and training in research methodologies, her high school courses also offered a critical ideological lens to science fields that seemed poignant for an inner-city school:

> My teachers would always tell us, like, you know, "Here are opportunities that you can take, so take them because this is the time when you're going to learn more and see." [. . .] I remember being told, like, women in science was just starting to emerge now. Like, it's usually men who are in the field, who are in abundance, and then a really—few women are able to succeed in the field. And, I thought, like, "Wow, why?" And, you know, that question has always been on my [mind] . . . like, why is it that women aren't able to progress in STEM fields? And *me*, since I'm a woman, too, trying to pursue a science major . . . That question is just in my head. Why is it that women are underrepresented in the STEM fields?

One of Natalia's teachers in particular emphasized the competitions in which students at the school were eligible to participate. As Natalia explained,

> She would want to get a lot of us into competitions . . . and there were some that were only for women . . . .She would always motivate the females in the room to participate in these competitions and not let that stop us from expanding our wings.

At the same time, Natalia explained, this teacher emphasized discrepancies in race/ethnicity: "I guess that was just her way of motivating us to keep going with our research. [She pointed out] the *minorities* . . . how they—how *we*—would be called in the STEM fields" and encouraged participation. Interestingly, Natalia did not recall instances in which discussions of the double bind of gender and race/ethnicity were explicitly discussed, nor did these arise in her high school internship experiences. By the time she and I began to speak, though, Natalia had grown quite aware of the double challenge she faced as both a woman and a member of the Latinx community.

As was briefly explained in Chapter 1, counterpsaces can play critical roles in enabling marginalized individuals to push against dominant narratives of exclusion or inadequacy. One of the most immediate ways in which counterspaces are enacted is through representation. Among the participants of this study, 38 percent of faculty mentors identified as Black, Latinx, or Asian. From the outset, Ruben, Anne, Natalia, and Amrita each saw themselves represented within the PRISM community, even if such representation was not as clear in the wider STEM disciplines. While not directly counteracting Ruben's and Anne's beliefs about grit, seeing themselves represented in a community of successful scientists contributed to the process of narrative identity work—the "process through which individuals or collectives give meaning to themselves and others through narratives" (Case & Hunter, 2012, p. 262). Counterspaces become important places where narratives about marginalized individuals can be contested, where members can push back against the "pejorative societal representations related to these individuals and their reference groups" (Case & Hunter, 2012, p. 262). Natalia saw herself clearly represented in the faculty, specifically choosing a female mentor who not only was a faculty member but also was raising a young family—a future Natalia envisioned for herself. Amrita, likewise, identified with her mentor as someone who, like her, understood how to get things done.

Up to this point, I have presented the initial disciplinary orientations of the students of color in my study. Equally important to consider are the perceptions of the two White women—both from low socioeconomic backgrounds and both first-generation college students. Chloe, who was interested in biology as well as forensic science, travelled two and a half hours each way to attend classes. Like Anne, she chose the college because of its affordability. Though originally she had wanted to attend a school in Boston, commuting from home was the "more affordable" option, even with the cost of daily bus tickets. Despite being in the honors program, Chloe struggled to see science as a discipline she could pursue, largely because of the costs and rigor of graduate programs. She pursued undergraduate research only as a means of fulfilling her requirements to graduate: "It's just easier for the fact that I don't have to commute to the city, then all over the city for an internship or something. It's just easier to stay at John Jay."

Chloe's orientation to scientific research was such that she expected to struggle, and she saw limitations to *who* can be a scientist (largely connected to economics and status). "It's not just like a high school lab," she explained; "it's a little intimidating because you're working with people with their PhDs and you're just the little undergrad." But at the same time, she was "excited" about the opportunity to be part of a research laboratory doing important work:

> I feel like, if you *can* be in science, you should use it for *good* science, and use it to help people. Like [my mentor] is doing. She's using this research to maybe guide doctors in some type of treatment. I feel, with science, you're supposed to help people, or you're supposed to help the planet. You're supposed to help with *something*. It sounds ridiculous to me to get some type of education and then just use it to make money.

Like Ruben, Chloe's altruism was palpable. As she explained to me, she felt enormous pressure from her immediate family to "go for something that will make money," but her desire to contribute to the good of the whole could not be suppressed. Also, like Ruben and Anne, Chloe's experience with regard to discrimination in science fields was limited. Chloe was aware that her mentor ran a program at the college for BIPOC women, but it was not something that was open to her as a White woman. "It's not something we usually talk about," she explained, "but it would be cool if we did. Actually, I hear more about stuff like that in my Lit classes . . . Like, the pay gap between women and men." Her only recollection of gender being discussed in the context of science was when a class discussed the discovery of the double helix: "The main thing the teachers even mention (and it's only briefly) is Rosalind Franklin. That's usually during lecture where they'll say, like, she was a brilliant scientist and didn't get the credit she deserved. But that's basically it." Race/ethnicity was never discussed.

As a computer science major, Madalyn's orientation to the field was slightly different from Chloe's. She had earned a degree in art at another institution years earlier, despite her interest in and aptitude for programming. For her, gender discrimination in computer science was far from hidden:

> I don't know if it has to do with being female. I think it does a little bit because I was very good at math when I was in middle school, and I had no problem understanding what I was looking at. I think when I got into high school, I got a little bit more self-conscious and wasn't interested in it, maybe, and then just stopped paying attention. I got okay grades, but suddenly I felt like I hated math. . . . When I went to college the first time, I was in art school—but it was an art school in a big technical university, so there were lots of [computer] guys there. They were just really unfriendly, socially awkward, kind of mean to girls and stuff. I just associated computer science with people who never got out and just liked playing video games—that sort of thing. I guess I just put it out of my mind. But at John Jay, there's quite a few girls in the computer science major. Girls who are

not dorks; who actually have social skills and are friendly. . . . I think there're a lot more girls that are interested in computer science and math and engineering, now, or that are pursuing it. They're encouraged to pursue it more now than in the past. It's just that [attending art school and then pursuing science] was a roundabout way of coming back to what I was originally interested in. I'm not blaming anybody . . . I don't regret having an art background and I feel like that's actually helping what I'm doing. It's enhancing what I'm doing.

Madalyn continued to speak about her experiences with computer science at the college, noting that students were not as competitive with one another as she had seen at other institutions, that they supported one another, that the faculty was diverse and there were female instructors (though mostly adjunct) who taught the computer science courses. But she was not completely naïve to the realities of the workplace. She explained that one of her female student colleagues at the tutoring center was also a computer science major:

> She's told me how she's encountered quite a few professors that she said were sexist and were trying to give her special treatment; were trying to make assignments easier for her and giving her easy As. She wasn't respected for her abilities. A lot of guys don't like the fact that there are girls learning how to program. They're very possessive over it and resentful. She's encountered a lot. When she has to work in groups, people will try to talk over her or she'll offer a comment or advice and nobody will listen to her. That sort of thing.

Despite these different orientations to the field of science broadly, none of the students in my study interpreted possible challenges and difficulties as being *institutionalized*—as something attributable to anything other than the residue of past discrimination, the rigor required to do good work, or the occasional "bad" instructor. They did not recognize how racism, sexism, or class could be woven into the fabric of how a community functions, its norms, or its discourse. All ascribed to a narrative of grit—if they worked hard enough and proved their abilities, they would be successful. There was no recognition that working hard might mean having to work *harder* than their White, middle-to-upper-class, male peers. Aside from Anne, none were aware that there might be differences in their academic preparation that could impact their performance; any fears about skill with math and science had been internalized as personal deficits. The invisibility of the reasons behind existing disparities meant that very few ever interrogated the *why* of it. It became too easy to make a false connection between lack of representation and lack of ability: "There aren't a lot of women and BIPOC in science because they aren't interested or capable." This thinking impacted not only how these student participants engaged with scientific spaces and artifacts, as examined in Chapters 3 and 4, but also how they navigated academic spaces broadly.

Considerations and Applications

It is easy, in the process of living our daily lives, to not notice what does not affect us as well as to attribute obstacles to causes other than what is truly responsible (much like we can talk away the symptoms of sickness as being due to stress or weather changes). It isn't until the challenges accumulate enough to create noticeable discrepancies that we begin to realize something is not right.

In this chapter, I have examined the ways in which White Institutional Presence has been institutionalized to the point of near invisibility as well as presented the orientations of program, faculty mentors, and students to STEM, broadly. In this exploration, I have also begun to unpack why it is necessary to turn our magnifying lens back onto ourselves, higher education, and our pedagogical and disciplinary practices. There will always be individuals who persist despite the added barriers, who will be held up as examples that anyone can accomplish anything if they have enough grit. But as educators, we must stop and ask ourselves why so many others do not make it through and what psychological effects linger as a result of that added hardship. We must ask ourselves what our pedagogical and disciplinary practices accomplish, where they might cause harm, and whether they can be accomplished through alternative approaches.

This chapter has largely served as the foundation for understanding the ways in which the day-by-day interactions between student researchers and faculty mentors impact not only disciplinary literacy in terms of understanding content and ways of knowing and being but also rhetorical skill development as a way of enacting disciplinary identity. In order to enact effective change, however, it is incumbent on members of disciplinary spaces to take stock of their practices and think about what will happen when students leave our classrooms and laboratories and begin to interact with other members of the discipline. How can disciplinary members change publication and review practices in their fields, for example? Or support female faculty as they transition into their own laboratories? This work needs to go beyond simply providing stipends and opportunities to do research. It needs to incorporate strategies for navigating hostile spaces when they are encountered and making meaningful changes when in positions of power.

Lifting the curtain on systemic bias is not only for the benefit of BIPOC and female students. Because of the invisibility of systemic bias, it is even more critical to do this work with White, male, and otherwise privileged groups who will not feel its effects. As part of educational frameworks, it is important to normalize examinations of the history of scientific practice and knowledge-making. Discussions about how research agendas and funding decisions are impacted by bias can be interwoven into methodology coursework and laboratory instruction.

Recognition of White language supremacy and linguistic bias in publishing can be integrated into discussions about how research findings are disseminated and can also be taken into consideration when designing disciplinary writing assignments and assessment rubrics. Explicit acknowledgment of gender bias in both publishing and career advancement can·be incorporated throughout a curriculum as can discussions about how to circumvent and dismantle such barriers. Avoiding discussions about the ways in which bias is systematized in disciplinary spaces only reinforces their invisibility, leaving it to students to interpret struggle as the result of an internal deficit.

In the next chapter, I extend the investigation of WIP in laboratory spaces through a lens of race-evasive ideology and microaggressions, continuing considerations of application. Race-evasion, or "color-blindness," allows meritocratic thinking to persist and for programmatic band-aids to be applied repeatedly without ever addressing the wound. Race-evasiveness also allows people to attribute differences in performance and ability to the individual, rather than to the systems in which that individual was raised. Because of this individualistic thinking, small slights or indirect, subtle remarks and actions can wear away at students' disciplinary identities and impact both their orientations to their fields and how they position themselves within those fields.

Chapter 3. The Psychosocial Costs of Race- and Gender-Evasive Ideologies

In the previous chapter, I presented White Institutional Presence (WIP) (Gusa, 2010) and discussed the ways in which it manifests in STEM educational spaces broadly and PRISM specifically. I also presented the orientations to STEM disciplines held by mentors as well as the research participants as they entered the program. In this chapter, I take a closer look at how these forces impact instructor ideologies and pedagogy and their effect on student writing and identity.

In his 2002 article, "The Linguistics of Color Blind Racism," Bonilla-Silva argues that "color blind racism, the central racial ideology of the post-civil rights era, has a peculiar style characterized by slipperiness, apparent nonracialism, and ambivalence" (p. 41). Color blind ideologies—or, to avoid ableist discourse, *race-evasive* ideologies—are those that position skin color and ethnicity as irrelevant or insignificant while ignoring the institutionalized systems that create and continue to reinforce racial inequality. They include the ideas that education is politically neutral and devoid of culture (Gay, 2010; Giroux, 1988; Shor, 1986), that to acknowledge difference is to reinforce divisions or to offer unfair advantages (Dee & Penner, 2017; Delpit & Dowdy, 2002), and that to cater to difference among student populations is to place barriers in their path toward successful assimilation into mainstream society—a belief that also rebuts the idea that to succeed in the mainstream often means mobilizing toward Whiteness, maleness, and middle-classness (Gay, 2010). These myths and misconceptions are the primary evidence Geneva Gay (2010) uses to support her argument that many educators—no matter how well-meaning—are "culture blind" and see "color-blindness" as a positive thing (p. 22).

Such ideologies manifest in language, pedagogy, and curriculum. Scholars such as Geneva Smitherman (1986), Keith Gilyard (1991), Jacqueline Jones Royster and Jean C. Williams (1999), and Vershawn Ashanti Young and colleagues (2018) have well-interrogated White meritocratic discourse in educational settings, including its impact on self-conception, academic performance, and educational policy. In their examination of White students' race-talk at a PWI, for example, C. Kyle Rudick and Kathryn B. Golsan (2018) identified how students' descriptions of "civil" academic discourse marked race-evasive ideologies as hallmarks of being a "good White person," which included the "expectation that students of color should talk like White students," emphasize race-based similarities over differences, and conform to expectations about what constitutes proper behavior in academic spaces (i.e., how individuals occupy space) (pp. 6–8). Mya Poe (2013), Asao B. Inoue and Poe (2012), Genevieve García de Müeller and Iris D. Ruiz (2017), and Staci M. Perryman-Clark and Collin Lamont Craig (2019) have also examined the impacts of discourse through studying the enactment of language instruction and assessment in writing programs and coursework.

Important to highlight is that race-evasive ideology is not necessarily a *conscious* mindset. While adopting a meritocratic stance—"You've made it to college, so you should be able to do these things"—ignores the systematic hurdles students have navigated to reach this point in their academic career, it is a common belief that permeates higher education. One part of race-evasiveness is believing that everyone entering college is at the same level and has had the same cultural resources, opportunities, and preparation. Ignoring or being unaware of systemic barriers that disproportionately impact BIPOC students constitutes race-evasion, just as ignoring or being unaware of barriers that disproportionately impact women is gender-evasive and those of first-generation and low-income students is class-evasive. These common and subtle forms of racism (and sexism, classism, etc.) form microaggressions that are, as Peggy C. Davis (1989) noted, "stunning, automatic acts of disregard that stem from unconscious attitudes of white superiority and constitute a verification of black [and female] inferiority" (p. 1576). Unchecked, microaggressions become part of the campus' racial and gendered climate and have negative impacts on academic spaces and underrepresented students (Solórzano et al., 2000).

Undergraduate research is often argued to be an important tool for retention and persistence initiatives for underrepresented students as well as for increasing disciplinary diversity. This thinking, though, necessitates that we imagine research as a space that is empowering and equal, that recognizes difference as power, and that is not *only* for the "exceptional" student who already sees a place for themselves in the field. When faculty members are working with underrepresented students in their disciplines, these considerations can become more salient—not because of any deficits in the student but because to ignore difference is to perpetuate inequity.

When students come to classrooms and laboratories, they bring their inquiry and enthusiasm; faculty mentors and educators bring research and expertise. By default, in these situations, a "third space" is created (Bhabha, 1994; Gutiérrez et al., 1999; Moje et al., 2004; Soja, 1996) that also includes "different instructional, home, and community knowledge bases and Discourses that bear on classroom [and laboratory] texts" (Moje et al., 2004, p. 41). It is important to think actively about these third spaces because there is a lot more going on there than people often realize. There is culture. There is ontology and epistemology—the ways people view the world differ from discipline to discipline and community to community. There is prior knowledge and history: history of the discipline, of the student's experience in academia, of the mentor's experiences as both a student and educator. As Moje et al. (2004) have argued, if the "social nature" of these different spaces are not acknowledged, "then the knowledges and Discourses generated in each seem to take on a life of their own, as if they are somehow natural constructions that exist outside human interaction and relationships" (p. 41).

These third spaces can function in multiple ways, but for the purposes of this chapter, we will consider them spaces with the potential to build bridges between communities (Gutiérrez et al., 1999), to cross disciplinary boundaries (Lemke, 1990; Moje et al., 2001), and to challenge dominant discourses (Barton, 2001; Moll & Gonzalez, 1994). When race-, gender-, and class-evasive ideologies persist, however, they form a disruption to this bridge-building and disciplinary understanding potential. Treating language as though it exists outside of communities is problematic for individuals from historically underrepresented groups because it does not recognize the socially constructed nature of discourse and reinforces WIP.

Disciplinary Literacy and the Construction of Excellence

When students are not aware of the ways in which systems of oppression impact how they engage with institutions of learning and disciplinary spaces, they often internalize challenges as being deficits within themselves. While I will explore what happens when instructors share such race- and gender-evasive ideologies later in this chapter, it is important to begin by looking at how in the early stages of undergraduate research systemic bias impacts the very mechanics of networking and gaining access and how that impact can affect disciplinary literacy.

Deborah Brandt (1998; 2015) has made clear and convincing arguments about the social aspects of literacy development, noting the roles sponsors play in regulating, sanctioning, permitting, and allowing access to the materials and spaces where such learning can take place. "Literacy," she argues, "like land, is a valued commodity in this economy, a key resource in gaining profit and edge" (1998, p. 169). For decades, there has been a recognition that STEM literacy is unequal across gender, racial, and economic categories, with a particular focus on access. When considering the "pipeline" students follow in STEM education, there are clear activities that often receive attention as being worthwhile in assisting retention and persistence of women and BIPOC students (despite outcomes being questionable regarding effectiveness). Such activities include increased programming around science and math in K-12 settings, networking and mentoring opportunities for high school and undergraduate students, and curricular support in math and science to aid students in strengthening needed skills. While such programs *do* play important roles in building access and opportunity, they ignore the systemic biases that are built into the epistemologies and practices of the STEM disciplines, and it is often expected or assumed that students who persist to the undergraduate research level have developed enough disciplinary literacy to be successful as junior members of the field. There are, as Cornelius Minor described in an interview with Sarah McKibben (2020), "pernicious ideologies" that persist in academia—ideologies that hold that when students reach a particular stage in their education, there are certain concepts they should know and certain behaviors they should display that reflect gratitude and deservedness of the opportunities afforded them. These ideologies become particularly salient when working with underrepresented individuals in STEM fields.

Some faculty mentors in this study, for example, expected students to "show initiative" and have clear goals of working toward graduate school. Students who were unclear of their career and academic possibilities, who were not entering the door articulating strong aspirational intentions, were dissuaded from "taking a spot" in the program. The intention behind this thinking was that students who *know* what they want should be provided the opportunities they need—with the unintentional consequence that those unsure or not already seeing themselves as worthy were left behind. By creating something "special," the program was also creating something exclusionary, replicating existing meritocratic systems.

While undergraduate research has been widely lauded as a high-impact practice that is transformative for STEM students, programs that provide undergraduate research opportunities are resource-intensive programs, requiring significant institutional costs—everything from preparing faculty to work with undergraduate students, to preparing students for the work of a real-life laboratory, to creating physical spaces with access to machines and materials for conducting research. R1 institutions benefit from economies of scale in hosting such programs due to increased funding opportunities, lower teaching loads, and higher prestige; HSIs and MSIs are among the least prepared in terms of financial support and laboratory infrastructure to offer such experiences to students (National Center for Science and Engineering Statistics, 2015). While institutional designations such as HSI and MSI means that these institutions can apply for racialized federal funding through programs like Title III and Title V (through the Department of Education), it also means that other non-racialized funding resources are much harder to secure. Further, as Nicholas Vargas (2018) notes, institutions with HSI status have "increased fivefold over recent decades, leading to greater competition between them for these racially designated resources" (p. 1). Vargas further highlights how, even amongst institutions designated as Hispanic-serving, those with "larger white and smaller Black student bodies are more likely to receive competitive funds" with (oddly) the proportion of Latinx students having no noticeable impact (Abstract). Such discrepancies—which Vargas noted are historically rooted in racial composition—reinforce existing disparities, and predominantly upper-class students preferentially benefit (Vargas & Villa-Palomino, 2019).

The uniqueness of a program such as PRISM existing at an urban, public HSI/MSI was not lost on the students or faculty. An aura of specialness surrounded the program and those who were admitted. Access to the program, for all of the student participants in this study, was considered an honor. While being part of something unique and special used to bolster students' sense of worth, it also had an unintentional consequence of creating an atmosphere of expecting "transactional gratitude." In an interview with McKibben (2020), Minor described transactional gratitude as follows: "In most academic spaces, there is a silent pact that teachers make with students: *I will agree to teach you well if you demonstrate to me that you are thankful for it. And if you do not demonstrate to me that you are thankful for it, I will withhold quality teaching from you*" (para. 10). On its surface, when faculty members are giving up research time to mentor newcomers, this expectation seems reasonable. Unlike in a classroom, students are not required to participate in undergraduate research and, as such, if they do not seem interested or willing to do the work (i.e., demonstrate thankfulness), then mentoring is not a worthwhile use of a faculty member's time. Problems with this ideology occur when our expectations of what constitutes engagement or thankfulness is normed on traditional STEM students.

One of the ways in which thankfulness presents is in the reading and writing work students do on their own time. Students who came to meetings with mentors having conducted some research into the work of the laboratory were interpreted as students who "put in the work" and showed initiative. Engagement with scholarly research translated as interest and preparedness. A discussion of how this plays out with students is offered later in this chapter, but it is important to note here that this ideology of being grateful for an opportunity like PRISM had immediate impacts on how students were positioned within the laboratory. Were they going to require a lot of "hand-holding," or could they be assigned low-stakes tasks right at the start? Did they need guidance on how to find and read peer-reviewed scholarship, or could they be given a topic for a literature review and be left to their own devices to work on it?

Connected to this positioning of academic-preparedness-as-thankfulness are considerations of race and gender. In their research on the experiences of Black women with the "white gaze" in the workplace, Verónica Caridad Rabelo and her colleagues (2021) diagram the ways in which "display rules" (ways of occupying and performing in spaces) are normed on Whiteness, focusing specifically on the ways in which Black women are consistently misread in professional spaces. For example, assertiveness in Black women is read as aggression (as in the Angry Black Woman trope), beauty standards and professionalism are based on Eurocentric aesthetics, and a lack of regular smiling is read as being threatening. While the students in this study did not consciously encounter these specific challenges in their PRISM laboratory experiences, some *were* regularly misread in ways that were similarly harmful.

Anne, for example, was a shy, young Black woman who was taught not to inconvenience her elders. She saw her mentor as a busy researcher who should not be disturbed unless necessary (someone who "had more important things to do"). As such, Anne would try to work out her research problems independently or wait until she had reasonable access to her mentor, Dr. Meijer. Dr. Meijer, however, read Anne as a student who required significant direction and supervision. At one point early in the study, Dr. Meijer commented that Anne did not seem to know what she was doing or why—a message that Anne received and internalized as evidence of not being ready for undergraduate research. This disconnect impacted everything in Anne's research experience—from their conversations about the scholarship Anne was reading to her physical access to the laboratory and materials needed for her project. As a result, Anne and Dr. Meijer pulled further apart rather than building a mentor-mentee bond.

As Marieke van den Brink and Yvonne Benschop (2012) outlined in their examination of gender and academic excellence, "excellence" is constructed on the spot through the recruitment and selection of individuals to be part of competitive programs and opportunities. This selection often relies on faculty and students having prior relationships (e.g., the student having taken a course with the faculty member), the student being known as a high-performing individual, or the student being friends with another peer who is already a member of the faculty mentor's laboratory (and who can serve as a reference). Selection is also impacted by a student's interest in pursuing graduate school, the amount of time they can devote to research, and their academic performance. At the time of this study, PRISM students were required to have successfully passed Organic Chemistry II, which served as a gatekeeping course (this requirement has since been changed to introductory courses), as well as have a grade point average of at least 2.5. Most mentors interviewed for this study reported having prior relationships with their mentees, primarily through coursework. At least half of the mentors reported self-selecting (inviting) students who did well in their courses to apply to the program.

This construction of excellence—who is *seen* as being an excellent student and potentially excellent undergraduate researcher—was based largely on academic performance and the performance of gratitude. There was no evidence that this selection process was impacted by physical appearance (gender, race, or class). Yet, that does not mean that the meritocratic thinking did not prevent mentors and program administrators from participating in "the production and reproduction of possible inequalities" (van den Brink & Benschop, 2012, p. 513). While I will investigate performativity as it relates to race, gender, and science in Chapter 4, it is worth noting here that it is in these relationships and in the interpersonal exchanges between mentor and student that messages about self-worth, belonging, and aptitude are conveyed.

As students enter undergraduate research, their mentor (and the program) becomes a literacy sponsor. As Brandt (1998) explained, when students move into new academic and disciplinary spaces, they are forced

> to consider not merely how one social group's literacy practices may differ from another's, but how everybody's literacy practices are operating in differential economies, which supply different access routes, different degrees of sponsoring power, and different scales of monetary worth to the practices in use. (p. 172)

In order to succeed in undergraduate research, students need to recognize that certain ways of communicating are expected of them. Part of the value of students participating in undergraduate research is that it provides a space for them to adopt and practice the reading, writing, and ways of knowing that are enacted in disciplinary spaces. Through access to a mentor, they gain access to knowledge of the disciplinary community: the forms of knowledge valued, the processes of inquiry, the rhetorical moves privileged, and the physical space and materials to engage in research activities. In this way, mentors become powerful literacy sponsors with regard to their discipline—i.e., they recognize that role as belonging to them. Strong relationships between mentor and mentee, where understanding is demonstrated regarding meeting students where they are (as opposed to where they "should" be), builds commitment and obligation to the URE and, as will become evident in the rest of this book, affects "what, why, and how [students] read" (Brandt, 1998, p. 198). A lack of commitment or obligation can lead to detachment and attrition.

How Mentors Learned to Read and Write as Scientists

In the early phases of this research study, I interviewed ten faculty mentors[6] in PRISM about the reading and writing practices of scientists. In addition to discussing the ways in which they learned to communicate in their respective fields, our conversations explored how that translated into their teaching practices. This section explores the ways in which these orientations to scientific discourse aligned with, or counteracted, White meritocratic discourse in science disciplines and, by extension, these mentors' pedagogical thinking regarding discourse instruction.

Of the ten mentors interviewed, all of them reported never having any form of formal pedagogical instruction during their graduate and postdoctoral career—none of them ever had a course related to teaching or a course related to scientific writing instruction. Eight out of ten of the faculty members reported that they learned to read and write as scientists in what they referred to as "the traditional manner."[7] They were told to write something—an abstract, a proposal, a paper summarizing results, etc.—and were given no instruction on what that was supposed to look like. They went off and did the writing, then received critical feedback after submitting to an advisor. Usually, that feedback was in the form of: "You're doing it wrong. Do it again." Or, in some cases, they received a lot of red marks on the page "correcting" their writing. Through trial and error, over time, they learned how to communicate in a way that was

---

6. Demographically, 40 percent of these mentors identify as male, 60 percent as female; 50 percent identify themselves as White, with the remaining 50 percent identifying as Black, Asian, and Latinx.

7. The use of the terms "traditional" and "nontraditional" refer specifically to how *scientists* learn the discipline and disciplinary discourse—this is the way these faculty members talked about writing. It is not reflective of traditions in writing studies.

acceptable to the scientific community. It is important to note that this was not a positive experience for many of these faculty mentors. The emotional trial this traditional learning process took on some of these scholars was traumatic. One mentor described the writing experience during her doctoral studies (which is where all of her science writing training came from) as a process of "ripping all of the confidence out of you."

Within the group who had traditional training in scientific writing, a portion had moments that disrupted the traditional approach—positively and negatively. The mentor who described herself as having all of the confidence ripped out of her as a writer had a member of her dissertation committee step in during the 11th hour to provide intense writing instruction. She said he sat beside her and they went through the text, line-by-line, to edit her thesis so that it would pass, and she credited him with providing most of her training in scientific writing. Others in this category noted a moment when a peer or a faculty member took time to break down the components of a specific writing project or provide genre instruction, such as the format of a scientific paper, for example. But other than these exceptions, in general, these faculty mentors had a traditional learning experience with regard to scientific writing. The remaining two faculty mentors—notably the mentors for Ruben, Natalia, and Amrita—had received what they referred to as "nontraditional" training in scientific communication. This included explicit instruction by a mentor on how to read scientific articles and extract information as well as on writing in various scientific genres and even included course supplements that focused specifically on disciplinary writing.

The two faculty who had a nontraditional writing education expressed positive relationships with the writing process and stressed the value of writing to scientific work, both in cognitive terms and communicative. For example, one faculty mentor spoke about the relationship of task-oriented writing (lists, etc.) to the final report or paper's organization, emphasizing the need to convey the *story* of the research. Another spoke about the implications of writing skill on a scientific career, equating the ability to write well with competence as a scientist.

When comparing the mentors' learning experiences with teaching, I noticed an interesting shift. Fifty percent of all faculty interviewed were using nontraditional teaching approaches for science writing instruction, such as guided readings, explicit teaching of genre and jargon, scaffolded assignments, and making sure to present scientific discourse as its own language. Of the ten faculty mentors interviewed, all declared that they were taught to write by trial-and-error. Only two faculty mentors noted having supplementary disciplinary writing instruction during their degree. Both types of mentors noted using nontraditional teaching approaches related to disciplinary discourse. Of the eight faculty with no guided writing instruction during their education, six self-identified as using nontraditional approaches.

Given that none of these faculty mentors took courses in pedagogy or writing instruction during their graduate and postdoctoral work, this was a noteworthy observation. Of the faculty members who learned to write as scientists in a traditional manner, without any nontraditional elements or disruptions, over half of them taught using some form of (what *they* called) nontraditional pedagogy. Assigning multiple drafts and providing some explicit genre and language instruction was a common approach. Of the faculty members who had a traditional education with some nontraditional elements and disruption, all of them taught using a nontraditional approach. Some of these faculty members explained that it was because they did not want to do to their students what was done to them; the trauma these faculty members experienced as students affected their pedagogy. All mentors who chose to teach differently than the way they were taught also happened to have participated in a college-sponsored series of writing across the curriculum (WAC) workshops.

Only four of the faculty members who had been taught with a traditional approach continued to teach with a traditional approach. Interviews with these faculty members reflected David Coil et al.'s (2010) findings that faculty do not devote much time to teaching disciplinary writing skills both because of the time required to teach disciplinary content and also because of their own underpreparedness in terms of how to handle writing instruction. Part of this underpreparedness has to do with "expert blindness." As Mitchell J. Nathan and his coauthors (n.d.) explained this concept, "the development of domain expertise leaves people largely unaware of the workings of their own expert behavior and the processes and learning experiences that led to its development" (pp. 5–6). In short, these faculty mentors either forgot what it was like to learn to read and write in their discipline, or they adopted a tough-love approach—"I was able to do it, so my students should be able to do it, too." Many of these faculty members also adopted an attitude that "good writing" is generic, transfers across contexts, and therefore is the purview of English departments.

It is important to pause here to note that these faculty mentors, in addition to having no pedagogy-focused coursework in their doctoral or postdoctoral training, also did not have training with regard to the ways in which race and gender discrepancies develop in STEM education. A notable few were involved in building PRISM from the beginning and were deeply aware of the effects of discrepancies, but their understanding of the causes of these discrepancies aligned with most targeted retention and persistence initiatives, which aimed to help students "catch up" through remediation and opportunities for research engagement. Being unaware of or ignoring the systemic nature of racism and sexism in STEM education created a program-wide race-evasive ideology that was unconsciously reinforced by many of the faculty in the program (regardless of their own race and gender identities). This ideology is noteworthy because the institution is a HSI and MSI with a high number of first-generation, multilingual, and low-socioeconomic status students. Those students whose mentors taught with the traditional approach reported that they were struggling with the discourse and feeling alienated from the discipline.

Cultural Expectations and Discourse

With the exception of one student (Natalia), all of the student participants in the study were new to the genres, language, jargon, and processes scientists use in their everyday work. Despite having taken core classes and the associated labs in their disciplines, five of the six students entered their undergraduate research experiences with little to no understanding of what was expected of them. For example, when Anne entered her mentor Dr. Meijer's lab, she had never read any scientific articles or books, short of textbooks. Her scientific writing experience, likewise, consisted of having only written laboratory reports for her organic chemistry course. When describing her approach to scientific writing in this context, she explained: "I write basically how I did it. . . . But, like, what I've learned at John Jay is that basically just say *why*. Just ask 'why?' Everything you do—say *why* . . . That is basically how you make a discussion." Her understanding of scientific writing at this stage was more aligned with academic assessment (i.e., laboratory notebooks for coursework) than with authentic disciplinary practice. Anne's understanding of genre conventions was also somewhat distorted. She understood that there was a reason, for example, that scientific papers and reports follow an Introduction, Methods, Results, and Discussion structure, but understanding what that reason was and executing that structure was challenging:

> The thing that really gets to me, though, is separating parts. It doesn't happen too much in chemistry, but in physics lab reports I tend to merge, so my Introduction tends to have a little analysis inside. And the analysis tends to have a little discussion inside. . . . So stuff are going where stuff are not supposed to be. I don't know why.

Because she was never taught to look for the rhetorical moves that occur in the different sections of a report and the subtle, but important, differences in stance, uses of evidence, presentation of data, and more in those sections, she was understandably confused and overwhelmed by this genre. Thus, Anne was at a disadvantage when entering Dr. Meijer's high-demand laboratory with little prior knowledge of or first-hand experience with the reading and writing practices of scientists (though, she at least had an awareness of this disadvantage).

Similarly, prior to writing her first proposal, Amrita noted that she was "not actually too sure what needs to go in there" and that she had a "general idea of how it's supposed to go, but [she didn't] really know how to write a proposal." Asking if she had an approach in mind for the writing process, Amrita responded: "I'll take quotes for what I need to and then organize [an outline] based on the quotes. And that's it. And major ideas that I need to talk about." In terms of anticipated revision, she was expecting possibly one large revision but nothing more substantial. These comments reflected that Amrita was neither clear on the discourse conventions of science disciplines (e.g., that direct quotations are not typical) nor on the rigor required to clarify one's ideas in such a discourse. Though the program did make available a template for the proposal, in this initial discussion, Amrita did not comment on planning to use it as a resource for her writing. She intimated that she was simply going to start putting ideas on paper (as she might for an English essay assignment) and then talk to her mentor, Dr. Bianchi, about what she should do next. Like Anne, at the start of her URE, Amrita was doing little more than experimenting with the discourse.

Similar experiences were documented with three of the other participants; Natalia was the one exception. Her experiences at an inner-city high school that focused specifically on STEM education through health and human services disciplines prepared her well for the reading and writing practices of undergraduate research. Her high school's approach to curricula and pedagogy embraced project-based, experiential and interdisciplinary learning, with a focus on providing "students with opportunities to learn about and understand how our independent global community functions and interacts" (Anonymous High School, 2017). At the same time, it made explicit the expectation that students would enter higher education after graduating and supported this expectation "by maintaining challenging academic standards and integrating education into professional settings so that [the students] acquire scientific knowledge, ethics, integrity and compassion" (Anonymous High School, 2017). In some of her early science courses at John Jay, Natalia noticed that students were "still learning how to break down a peer-reviewed journal article," which was something she had learned to do in high school. She was already quite comfortable with navigating articles to "see if it relates to your [research] topic" and finding what she needed in the various sections. This prior experience also helped with her writing-intensive science courses that involved writing pre-laboratory and post-laboratory notes, formal reports, and article summaries.

I begin by describing these experiences to establish a reality that I have written about elsewhere (Falconer, in press). These students had, effectively, passed the instructor expectation threshold in reading and writing for coursework (Sommers and Saltz, 2004), meaning they had met or exceeded the baseline needed to successfully engage with the genres, reading practices, and writing practices common to classroom instruction: short lab reports, identifying correct answers on a multiple choice test, composing effective open-answer exam responses, etc. They had arrived, so to speak. But as research has shown (e.g., Middendorf and Pace, 2004; Wilder, 2012), specific disciplinary ways of thinking and communicating are part of the hidden curriculum—often assumed by college instructors and not made explicit to students. As such, students moving from coursework to undergraduate research encounter a new, unexpected threshold despite disciplinary continuity. Highlighting the instructor expectations for PRISM students as they entered their respective UREs helps illustrate one aspect of this threshold and how WIP plays a role or is subverted.

For example, Amrita and Natalia's mentor, Dr. Bianchi, viewed the reading and writing practices of scientists as a language and practice unlike any other. At the time of this study, Dr. Bianchi was an early career faculty member at the college. In our first conversation, I was struck by how cognizant she was of the rhetorical challenges newcomers to science face, particularly women, multilingual students, and students of color. She spoke of how the language of science is quite particular and of how the discourse of her subfield, specifically, is very much in flux. Like Dr. Meijer (Anne and Madalyn's mentor), her perception of poor writing and reading skills on the part of students at the college frustrated her, but Dr. Bianchi chose to take up the challenge by meeting students where they were and incorporating writing instruction into her coursework. She participated in college-sponsored WAC seminars, designed writing-intensive courses, and took a scaffolded approach to teaching disciplinary rhetorical practices within her laboratory. Dr. Bianchi was emphatic that writing is "absolutely integral" to the work of science, saying, "If you can't write, you're useless as far as I'm concerned. And if you can't write well, then you don't succeed. I mean, to me it's pretty clear-cut. It sets apart the successful scientists from the non-successful ones." Both students saw in Dr. Bianchi an individual who would actively mentor them, who was interested in getting to know them as people, and who was not only patient but also a strong scientist. Dr. Bianchi's approach to mentoring also took into account both students' skills and interests, leaving room for Amrita and Natalia to grow at their own pace.

Though Amrita was not aware of it, at the beginning of her URE, Dr. Bianchi had already started her on many of the prewriting tasks required for the successful writing of proposals. In particular, Dr. Bianchi assigned Amrita to read a series of scholarly materials related to the work being done in the laboratory—mostly journal articles, but interestingly also Dr. Bianchi's doctoral thesis. In addition to the thesis, some of the articles had been written by Dr. Bianchi herself. This was largely because her discipline is a "baby field," as Dr. Bianchi described it, and there simply was not much scholarship to reference. Dr. Bianchi's research was breaking new disciplinary ground. But as I learned later, she expected (and explicitly directed) that her thesis be used as a model *as well as* a content resource by Amrita. In one-on-one meetings, Amrita had the opportunity to ask questions about the content and scientific processes as well as bring up any elements she did not understand. The primary challenge in this reading, Amrita noted, had to do with language: "I didn't really know the language that they used and I wasn't too sure how they were doing things." Adding to this complication was the fact that the terminology used (including some *she* would need to use) is still evolving and under great debate.

In addition to the research articles and thesis, Dr. Bianchi required Amrita to review disciplinary textbooks, which included a significant number of images, particularly photographs. Because Amrita was going to be observing animal growth, it was critical that she understood the various stages of development and what these actually *looked* like. Dr. Bianchi followed this reading up by personally taking Amrita into the lab and showing her specimens. As Dr. Bianchi noted, the practice of reading coupled with discussion of those readings and first-hand exposure to the process itself (e.g., looking at the stages of development in the lab) helps students

> to pick out the important things and [gets] them to critically evaluate work that's out there. So, kind of mold them and get them to pick out things like: "What makes a good experiment versus what makes a not good experiment?" And, "You know in the Discussion section—do you think that maybe they should have considered this?" And "Going through the experimental design, where do you think some more errors could have been?" So all of that kind of comes up in discussing the paper, and [the students] usually evolve and are able to pick up things like that on their own after a couple months.

In the early stages of research, Dr. Bianchi put a heavy emphasis on reading rather than writing, though she did take time to instruct students on how to create and complete data sheets and keep a "side notebook" to document everything they noticed in the lab. Though she did not describe it in these terms, it was clear that Dr. Bianchi saw the data sheets as a "fuzzy genre" (Medway, 2002) and made sure her students saw it as such, as well:

> What I've learned is you have a data sheet and you really don't know if it works properly or not until you are halfway through the experiment and you realize that it doesn't. So, at least you have your notebook that you're writing down the additional information. So if you have to run the experiment again, you update your data sheet and make it more functional.

To that end, Dr. Bianchi provided students with a binder in which she expected them to put a paper copy of each article they read related to the project, the data sheets, and then additional notes and observations. She also kept a stack of sticky notes handy for drawing Venn diagrams, life cycles, and points to remember that could easily be attached to a page in the binder. These practices directly mirrored her own document collection and writing practices. These papers, data sheets, and notes all formed the basis for the students' research proposals because students were often well into research before funding proposals were submitted. Dr. Bianchi did not guide the initial writing of Amrita's proposal except to note that she should use Dr. Bianchi's thesis as a model for form (not length). As such, Amrita was left to synthesize the information she had learned as a mentee and translate it into a document.

Amrita submitted this draft to Dr. Bianchi, who commented *heavily* in the margins as well as line edited the text. When asked how she felt when she opened the digital file, full of blue text edits and comment boxes, Amrita responded:

> So, I did not expect that. Like, I would not expect that heavy of edits. And especially the first submission that I submitted for the abstract was like—basically every word was edited, pretty much every single sentence. So, I didn't expect that at all. But it was great. It was great to be able to compare what I did to what she rewrote and how she rewrote it. My content was there. It was my delivery of it, that was what she tweaked a lot of.

Though many students would understandably be intimidated and, possibly, disheartened by the amount of edits on that first draft, Amrita's strong sense of self and self-positioning as a learner helped her to look past any rejection and to the substantial learning opportunity available. This was bolstered by Dr. Bianchi's positioning of the discourse itself. Dr. Bianchi used this as a teaching opportunity; her comments and edits were rich with information about the subset of the scientific discourse community involved and the genre of the research proposal in general. For example, in the abstract of the proposal, Dr. Bianchi provided such comments as, "In [our field] we are shifting our terminology to reflect that we don't estimate PMI directly, all we can do is estimate the minimum time of colonization," and, "You want to also introduce a statement about the importance of biomarkers here." In this way, she was framing the discourse for Amrita in a way that pointed out rhetorical conventions of the field rather than positioning these as errors on the student's part. In modelling the discourse and providing an explanation for the changes, Dr. Bianchi was providing insights into how the discourse in the field was evolving; what that meant in terms of scientific practice; and importantly, how these realities should be conveyed through language. Throughout the first edited draft appeared similar comments, sometimes explicit instruction into practices such as using species names ("The first time you mention a species in a paper you need to include the full name and who named it"), sometimes clarifications on techniques or tools ("You are going to use containers, not jars"), and sometimes on needed additions to the text ("State here how the specimens are placed on filter paper . . . ").

During the revision of this first proposal, Amrita was tasked with doing additional, independent reviews of the scholarly literature to flesh out various aspects of the proposal. Though this was at times challenging, she felt the recursive process of writing and reading was helping her to become an expert on her own. And the work certainly paid off. When she submitted the second revision of her proposal, much of the new text Amrita added to flesh out the introduction was unedited by Dr. Bianchi (excepting comments on the need to cite certain claims). In this second version, Dr. Bianchi's focus shifted from large-scale organizational requests to requests for greater specificity and additional examples in the literature review and for the inclusion on definitions where necessary. The feedback had moved from larger genre concerns to more narrow disciplinary conventions. By the fourth draft, the edits Dr. Bianchi requested were limited to small line edits on two different pages, focusing on preferred semantics that improved sentence flow but that did not change meaning. The final (fifth) version Amrita submitted to Dr. Bianchi was approved without edits.

After she successfully received her first research stipend, with a strong positive response from the program coordinator, I asked Amrita how she felt about the scientific "voice" and if it was something she felt comfortable with or if it was awkward. Her response was one of laughter, followed by seriousness:

> Um, I think it's not necessarily either one of those. I think it's just like foreign. It's like, it's not—I feel like after I've gotten used to it, after I understand it, it will make more sense. It's starting to make sense after these writings that I've done. But, like, I'd never read any [scientific articles] or like written anything with that [before now], so it's just like, you know, I didn't know what to expect. I didn't know how to write it, that's all. I feel like once I get used to it, once I do more of them, it's not going to be as big of a deal.

By positioning scientific discourse as a foreign language that had to be learned, systematically, rather than as an extension of typical academic writing in English, Dr. Bianchi helped Amrita successfully sidestep a situation in which she might consider herself as deficient or underprepared. Similarly, Dr. Bianchi's mirroring of Amrita's abilities to succeed through the types of comments and instruction she offered, positioned Amrita as a burgeoning scientist that simply needed explicit instruction in the discourse of her sub-discipline rather than someone who was incompetent or unable to handle the work.

At the start of her undergraduate research experience, Natalia described Dr. Bianchi as "so willing to tell me about the projects and what's going on." At the same time, Dr. Bianchi made sure to let Natalia know that she was not expecting her to understand everything she was "throwing" at her, reassuring Natalia that she would send her everything she would need to get ready for research and training. Natalia described the situation as follows:

> When I was hearing her tell me all of these projects, inside of me I just thought, "How am I going to do this?" Because I don't know all of this that is going on. Like, I've done a bit of research, but it hasn't been enough for me to understand all of these projects in detail. But when she told me, "I'm going to give you all the information you need," I was a lot more calm and like, "Okay, I can do this. I can do this."

As with Amrita, Dr. Bianchi's first step with Natalia was to send her scans of a textbook and copies of research articles that were relevant to the research being conducted in the laboratory. She instructed Natalia to "just try to comprehend as much as [she could] about what would be in her research, because . . . those are the basics that [she] would need." Dr. Bianchi explained that once Natalia had a chance to read through the materials, they would sit down together and talk through the research, then decide on next steps for the proposal. Though there was only a month from this initial meeting until the time the proposal was due to the PRISM office, Natalia was confident: "I feel like once the positive environment is set with a mentor even if the deadline's coming up, the contact with the mentor will help get that proposal done."

At this early stage, Natalia was not sure how she was going to approach the proposal writing process because she was not sure which project she would be working on. But she was confident that once they had formally decided on a topic for research, "the writing part will be easier." Though she had prior experience with a scientific research proposal, this would be the first proposal Natalia would write for PRISM. She had reviewed PRISM's guidelines, noting that "they looked pretty intense." At the same time, she saw in the guidelines a useful template. She explained that her process would involve creating an outline using the requirements as a guide, drafting the sections throughout, and then revising the proposal as a whole so that it would become more cohesive—"that way there is a flow in my writing."

Natalia and Dr. Bianchi met again not long after this initial meeting and discussed the research papers and potential projects. They decided on the project Natalia would be part of, which allowed her the space to get started on the proposal. Before starting to write, Natalia met with PRISM's program coordinator to talk about the writing expectations. She described that meeting thus:

> I don't want to seem like I'm laid back about my scientific writing . . . .So, he said, "Oh, you know, don't worry about it. Write as if you're writing to me or if you were writing to a couple of friends who don't know what's going on, so you have to be . . . you have to explain it." . . . He told me, "As long as you're able to communicate to me what the experiment you're doing [is] and how it's important to your community, then I'm pretty sure you're going to do a good job with it." [. . .] I took his words into consideration and I thought, "Ok, let me just write it like as if I was writing to a friend rather than, I guess, the scientific community," because that's what [he] was talking to me about doing. So I did that, but I wasn't—I wasn't satisfied with what I did. So I tried to incorporate a lot more scientific terms and like the, specifically the names of the [organisms] that we're specifically looking at. Then I changed it a lot.

Though Natalia had gotten clear direction from the program coordinator about the audience and tone for the proposal, it was in direct opposition to what she had already absorbed as appropriate scientific discourse. As noted earlier, Dr. Bianchi had provided all of the students in her laboratory with a copy of her doctoral thesis to act as both a content reference and a writing model. In approaching this first proposal, however, Natalia wanted to start more autonomously:

> I thought, "Okay, let me do a draft on my own without taking a look at hers . . . at her thesis." So I wrote down, you know, the basics of me being in the lab and keying out the [organisms] or the species that we—that [Dr. Bianchi]—had collected. But then I thought, "Okay, this needs to have a lot more information that I wouldn't be able to get if I *didn't* look at her thesis.

Looking at the thesis meant that Natalia noticed the specificity of the language Dr. Bianchi used and that there were significant differences in how Natalia was describing equipment and objectives and how Dr. Bianchi described them. Natalia observed, "It's one word, so [you] wouldn't think that it would be much of a difference. But it does."

As she worked through the proposal writing process, Natalia drew on her metacognitive skills about science writing, continuously checking what she was being told by the program coordinator and the proposal guidelines against what she knew from experience and then comparing these to the models of writing Dr. Bianchi had provided. Yet, despite drawing on this rich writing-knowledge bank, Natalia was still unsure about whether she was composing for the appropriate audience. Though she sent the first version to Dr. Bianchi for review, she did so with the explicit caveat that she was aware that this was not "100 percent scientific" and was pretty "bare." Dr. Bianchi agreed with Natalia and assisted her in revising the proposal to include even more specifics about the specimens themselves, the purpose of the research, and the methods and materials used. Dr. Bianchi's guidance to Natalia, however, did not focus on discourse conventions as it had with Amrita early on—instead Dr. Bianchi encouraged Natalia to do what she already knew how to do: "She was like, 'Oh, why don't you try to be a little more specific . . . and she put some suggestions on the draft" (such as [equipment] names and distinctions about procedures). In this way, Dr. Bianchi validated the background and knowledge Natalia brought to the lab from her high school experience.

Approaching the revisions, Natalia attempted to embody Dr. Bianchi's voice: "I thought, 'Ok, this is something [Dr. Bianchi] would say.'" Part of this approach drew on her time speaking with and listening to Dr. Bianchi, and part of it drew on the thesis Dr. Bianchi provided as a resource and model. When Natalia completed revisions, Dr. Bianchi reviewed the draft and responded, "That one's pretty good. Let's leave it at that."

By creating a laboratory environment in which students were recognized for the skills and experience they brought to the space but supported in new efforts, Dr. Bianchi served as an effective and valuable literacy sponsor while fostering a culture of growth and belonging. Students recognized that reading and writing (like the research process itself) is a recursive process that is not done alone. Dr. Bianchi's explicitly acknowledging these concepts meant that students were clear on the expectations for their performance; they had to work hard, but they were not in it alone. This meant that, regardless of their cultural capital or lack thereof upon entering the space, all students were set up to thrive.

This was a very different environment from other laboratory spaces in the program, however. For example, Anne and Madalyn's mentor, Dr. Meijer, was clear in interviews that she privileged self-directed learners and that she had no interest in mentoring students who were not looking to be scholars. "One of the first things I say when they meet with me," she explained, "is that if they are not thinking about publishing, they should not join my lab." She was also very clear about the type of students she wanted: "I tell them that they need to come to me with solutions, not problems." She directed interested students to a page on her lab website that gave potential mentees both practical advice (e.g., to delay trying to join the lab if they were over-committed with coursework or other activities), as well as warning students about her approach to mentoring ("A sharp and quick mind cannot take the place of hard work," and "If your adviser had the answer she would have published it already.") Whether conscious of this or not, Dr. Meijer was seeking students who had already positioned themselves as belonging within science as scientific researchers, students who had already recognized that they had valuable contributions to make and expected others to see them as professionals. Dr. Meijer was not interested in mentoring students who could not problem solve; she did not want to accept students who would email or text basic questions throughout the day or who required too much handholding. As Anne explained in an early interview, "She knows you're in this lab, you're big enough, you're *supposed* to know . . . to pace yourself and produce results." Dr. Meijer wanted future scholars who would step up to the challenge of research. In many ways, she was asking students to *be* scientists upon arrival without necessarily enabling those identities in the early stages of the URE. This approach, she conceded, had a lot to do with her own experiences in academia. Her experiences at the undergraduate level, she recounted, were particularly competitive, harsh, and at times humiliating. Students were expected to self-teach, and much of the examinations for coursework were public and oral (with high stakes). One either performed or they failed. And if they failed, they were publicly directed to other majors.

At the same time, Dr. Meijer was an incredibly open and welcoming individual whom both mentees in this study adored at the start of the study. In an early interview about mentoring practices, she described an intentionally designed, scaffolded approach to introduce students to the lab. In recounting her approach, Dr. Meijer described teaching new lab members how to effectively use the internet and databases to find scholarly material, including the use of Boolean searches. She claimed to teach students how to build literature reviews and assess sources. She demanded that they write their project protocol (the Methods and Materials section) before any other parts of the proposal and that they visit John Jay's writing center not once, but twice, to ensure clarity and coherence, even asking many to purchase themselves a copy of Strunk and White's *The Elements of Style* for reference. All of these components illustrated an awareness of how to enculturate new student researchers to the lab, even if there was little evidence during my study to show that these activities actually took place. (They may have occurred in prior years, however, or been enacted disparately.)

In short, Dr. Meijer was (in theory and intention) investing in the content knowledge of her mentees as well as in the practical, mechanical aspects of scientific writing. But she was also unintentionally reinforcing WIP in science and in academia broadly. Her expectations about self-efficacy and self-directed learning, students' understanding of the profession of science, and students' ability to answer questions for themselves through inquiry assumed a particular level of education and autonomy that many students from underrepresented backgrounds and underfunded communities do not possess. Culturally, such expectations assume that students will be comfortable with what they might see as challenging authority or imposing on others: making independent decisions without the explicit direction of a superior, persistently following up with a mentor on unanswered questions, etc. Because her expectations were not aligned with Anne's cultural capital at the start of the URE, a fertile ground was created for the two not understanding one another and for "reading" one another's abilities and intentions inaccurately.

Anne's response to this situation was to see herself as unprepared, unskilled, and unclear about how to move forward in research. Anne never received the rhetorical introduction to research that Dr. Meijer had described—she was not taught what a literature review was nor how to compose one, how to read or review a scientific article, or the various forms of writing she might encounter in the laboratory space. Anne remarked that she had a memory of one optional group instruction on using referencing software, but it was scheduled for a time when she was unable to attend. One-on-one instruction or make-up sessions never took place, and it was never clear to her why such a workshop would be of benefit to her work and scholarship. Similarly, Anne was left to herself to identify a potential research project at the start of the URE. For the first few weeks, she observed and assisted laboratory peers in their research, not understanding that she was supposed to be coming up with both a research question and a proposal to submit to PRISM for funding. She realized this needed to be done less than 48 hours before the deadline for submitting a proposal.

In order to help Anne make this deadline and acquire funding, Dr. Meijer strongly guided her toward a project to propose, rather than having her generate a topic independently. Dr. Meijer also provided Anne with a paper on similar work to reference and to guide her understanding, though because of the 11th-hour situation, Anne had not had an opportunity to read it before writing her proposal (thus missing critical information). Anne described the project to me hesitantly:

> I [will be trying to] retrieve viral particles—DNA and RNA
> phages—from bones that have been . . . that have been left . . .
> you could just say left out in the wilderness. Been left on . . .
> I don't know, what's the word I'm looking for? Untouched? So
> that's basically what I'm working on. And I'm going to be using
> pigs. Domesticated pigs to see if . . . I would have to look up
> internal viruses that are known to domesticated pigs, and then
> retrieve the bones to see if those viruses are present or are still
> present in the bones after, like, a period of let's say two months?
> Or, I don't know, sometime after. After all the decay and all of
> that has occurred.

Though she was enthusiastic, it was clear from her description that even after *writing* the proposal Anne was not sure what her project was about or how it would be implemented. Did she need to look up viruses first? Infect the pigs? Or were the pigs infected prior to arriving at the lab? How was the testing going to be conducted? These were questions she was not able to answer clearly in that discussion of her research, and she frequently confused the names of procedures and instruments. It appeared at that early stage of the URE that Anne's performance of "scientist" in discourse was unconvincing. She was also, as Dr. Meijer intimated in an interview, a perfect example of the "average student" encountered in her faculty role: lacking skill in communicating, in both oral and written forms; lacking a strong vocabulary in science; and having poor mathematical abilities. Fortunately, Dr. Meijer attributed these challenges to poor public schooling in the US and did not see them as deficits originating in the students themselves—though she did suggest that it was the students' responsibility to remediate these discrepancies, which ultimately, I believe, influenced Dr. Meijer's interpretation of Anne's work in the laboratory.

The proposal writing *process* was similarly disjointed. Anne struggled to get and keep a meeting time with her mentor due to Dr. Meijer's demanding schedule. Unfortunately, Anne also waited to work on the proposal until speaking with Dr. Meijer in person because she was, essentially, waiting to be told what to do. She did not feel she had the authority to write and propose ideas for research in someone else's lab without having discussed the possibilities first. Her reference points in orienting to the URE (as discussed in Chapter 2) were skewed, and she was struggling to understand the social contracts at play in the space. This resulted in the drafting of the entire proposal from scratch at the last minute:

> I did write a draft. I didn't get to write it as best as I could because
> I wrote it the night before the [due] date. Not because—Like I
> said, she was busy. I had that meeting with her the 22nd and
> I was like, "Do you want me to submit a proposal, because I
> know the deadline, it's so late?" And she's like, "Go ahead!" So

> basically the night of the 23rd I had to write. I was up 'til like
> four o'clock in the morning writing a proposal. Then I sent it
> to her in the morning, she reviewed it, sent me my corrections,
> sent it back to me, and then I submitted it that night. . . . I could
> have done it better . . . .I didn't read the paper that she gave me
> because I was against time. And I had to sleep. So I, like, I glazed
> over it. But when she sent me the reviewed version, I decided
> to take a look at [the paper], like revising my parts. And then
> I realized what I did for my results and what they had for their
> results was completely different from what they *actually* had!
> And I was like, "Oh my goodness!" So had to rewrite that whole
> part [before submitting it].

The feedback she received from the program coordinator on the submitted draft was helpful, though slightly disheartening. "Most of my errors were because of my lack of knowledge," she explained; "I really didn't know what I was doing. I knew what the end result should be, but I didn't know how I was going to get there." Though she was ultimately funded for this research project, Anne left the experience feeling inadequate. She interpreted her mentor's lack of attention as related to her, rather than Dr. Meijer simply being too busy. As Anne began her first research project, she was left with doubts about whether she belonged. When it came time to write a proposal for the next semester's funding cycle, she reported feeling "depressed and overwhelmed."

Madalyn (a White woman in her early thirties), who was also a member of Dr. Meijer's laboratory, had a very different level of cultural capital. Hers more closely aligned with her mentor's in that she actively sought out projects and answers for herself, conferred with Dr. Meijer only when necessary (but "hunting" her down when queries went unanswered), and taught herself software and techniques that would improve her performance in research. What Madalyn knew, but Anne was unaware of, was that "rules are negotiable" (Keels, 2019) and that, though the laboratory was technically Dr. Meijer's, as a member of the research community, she had leeway in terms of her process of inquiry. Autonomy was not only encouraged, it was expected. Anne also did not understand that Dr. Meijer would not view persistence as a problem; what Anne determined would be annoying (e.g., waiting outside Dr. Meijer's classroom to speak with her) was viewed by Dr. Meijer as dedication and showed a commitment to undergraduate research.

Though Madalyn had never taken a course with Dr. Meijer, never "had any contact with her" at all, she had met another student during the research training workshop who was already working in Dr. Meijer's laboratory. Madalyn was entranced by the kinds of research taking place there and, after "looking her up" to learn more about her work, wasted no time in reaching out:

> I was like, "I want to do that!" And I basically—you know she's
> very busy, so I had to chase her down. I was very persistent and

she's like, "It's pretty crowded in the lab." And I was like, "Well, I'll find something to do." She's very welcoming. . . . She just hasn't told anybody "no." I think she thinks that people will filter themselves out. Like, if they're not genuinely interested, they're just going to stop showing up. So, it kind of takes care of itself. . . . I just felt like I had to work with her.

Whereas Anne perceived Dr. Meijer's allusiveness as evidence that she did not belong in the laboratory, Madalyn saw it as a challenge—going so far as to wait outside Dr. Meijer's classroom for a chance to speak to her about research opportunities. Madalyn was not intimidated by Dr. Meijer at all, and this was my first glimpse into her ability to compartmentalize. Over the course of my research, I was consistently impressed with Madalyn's ability to focus on the objective at hand and block out the social factors that might have dissuaded other students. "I think," she explained, "once I get an idea in my head, if I don't do it, then I'm annoyed at myself. I guess it's just the attitude, 'What have I got to lose?'"

Madalyn wasted no time in bringing herself up to speed on the work happening in the laboratory. As soon as Dr. Meijer gave her permission to join the laboratory, Madalyn began reading—first a grant proposal Dr. Meijer was preparing to submit, then independently-sourced material. "We do a *lot* of research in the literature about the experiments that we want to do," she explained, "and the procedures we want to follow, and trying to get ideas. So, that's where I am right now." Using John Jay's library, Madalyn began searching the databases to learn more about the types of work taking place in Dr. Meijer's laboratory. "You can look things up by journal," she explained,

but if I'm looking for a particular subject, I can type that in and it'll call up every scientific [article] that has a phrase that you're looking for. So, usually, I end up looking in the *Journal of Forensic Science, Analytical Chemistry, Biochemistry*, archeological scientific journals. . . . It can be a rabbit hole. One thing leads to another, and all these papers reference each other, so you end up going to references, and then the references have references. . . .

Though this was the first time she had conducted scientific research, Madalyn was able to effectively draw on the skills she had learned in her earlier educational experiences to successfully navigate the databases and find content relevant to the work of the laboratory. Importantly, she had very quickly developed an understanding of the specific academic journals that would be of use to her.

Prior to this experience, like most of her peers, Madalyn had never read a scientific paper, and found her first attempts overwhelming. "When I first read a scientific paper," she explained, "I was like, 'I don't understand what any of this means! This language is totally foreign to me. It's so dense and so complicated.' But the more I read, it's getting so much better to understand what's going on."

Though (like Anne) Madalyn did not have any direct instruction on reading scientific materials, during the first half of that semester, the genre conventions of the scientific article became apparent through repeated exposure, which made navigating the pieces more manageable. "It's like a standard format that everyone has to follow," she explained. "You treat it like a sandwich. You read the beginning [the Introduction] and then the end [the Results and Discussion], and then the middle [the Methods]. That makes it nice and easy for me to understand." This strategy allowed Madalyn to "extract the important points" in an efficient manner. As she read, she kept a notebook with entries related to each article, making connections to other pieces of literature. It was clear that, in a short period of time, Madalyn had adapted her prior knowledge of academic research practices to develop a sophisticated approach for reviewing the scientific literature. She never questioned whether she was allowed to propose new lines of inquiry, nor did she worry that she was pushing the established boundaries within the lab. Rather, in many ways, her autonomy and strong sense of belonging created a sense of ownership and entitlement to the space.

Despite this progress, Madalyn held off writing her research proposal until she had a fully formed idea and, as a result, missed the cutoff for funding for the spring semester. Instead, she began writing a proposal to be considered for summer funding, using her time in the spring to work through the ideas and conduct a more thorough review of the literature. Surprisingly, this additional time to think through the project, and her observation of how much time it took for an animal carcass to decompose, resulted in a major directional shift:

> I was involved in two different projects [for Dr. Meijer], and I decided to focus on one that was more practical for me to accomplish things with. There was one that involved computer science, developing software, machine learning software. And then the other one was looking at bone trauma on cremated remains—which is a really interesting field, but there was really no way to [conduct] enough experiments for me to feel like I was doing something. . . . I like to be active. . . . I decided to change direction and focus on the machine learning software, which is—I'm NOT a computer science student. I have very little knowledge about it. . . . But the long-term goal of the project is to construct software that will recognize features that you photographed on something, like human bones.

Though there was already a graduate student working on this project, Dr. Meijer and Madalyn agreed that this was an appropriate project for her to assist on. And, despite her emphatic resistance at the start of the URE to any identity as a computer scientist, Madalyn was able to see a connection between the work the laboratory conducted, the role of photography in evidence gathering (which referenced her art background), and her confidence in her ability to learn new technology and skills.

The difference in how Anne and Madalyn each experienced the same laboratory was noteworthy and is reflective of how many underrepresented students internalize challenges as a deficit in them rather than as a failure of those in charge to articulate the rules and expectations of the space. On one hand, we can view these interactions as part of the "weeding out" process that Madalyn noted. On the other, we can view it as the enactment of WIP in STEM education: assimilate or leave, show gratefulness for this opportunity or receive less attention. At the URE level, this is problematic, because some students are only beginning to understand the practices and habits of mind of their respective fields and because that assimilation process could also be weeding out innovative and potentially strong researchers.

The orientations students hold within an academic space also have profound impacts on whether they feel comfortable composing in and for that space and on the authority that they demonstrate in their writing. Anne's work (both in oral description and written drafts) illustrated an insecurity with the ideas and practices of the research, embodied by hedges, incorrect terminology, and lack of detail. She was uncomfortable almost to the point of paralysis. Madalyn, on the other hand, was able to claim a niche for herself and take risks, knowing that her mentor would correct any misunderstandings or incorrect terminology use. UREs place incredible literacy demands on students, which can be mitigated through mentorship as well as through clear articulations of expectations for performance and explicit instruction on disciplinary discourse conventions (see Chapter 4). As faculty mentors and educators, we need to question whether our policies and expectations are having the unintentional consequences of losing valuable talent and minds.

Considerations and Applications

Despite inclinations to view educational and disciplinary spaces as arhetorical and apolitical, it is critical to recognize that pedagogical practices in teaching disciplinary norms and discourses are infused with preconceived ideas of what it means to be an "excellent" student and worthy of educators' time and energy—ideas that can have roots in racial, gender, and class inequities. Ignoring (or being ignorant of) race- and gender-evasive ideologies can have significant impacts on students' self-concepts and sense of belonging in the discipline.

When considering disciplinary writing instruction, it is critical to remember that discourse is part of culture and a *reflection* of culture (Gee, 2001). It is something that needs to be taught explicitly. As Ahmed (2006) has noted, the arrival of students in the classroom

> is dependent on contact with others, and even *access* to the "occupation of writing," which itself is shaped by political

> economies as well as personal biographies. . . . Having arrived,
> [a student] might do a different kind of work given that [they]
> may not put these other attachments "behind" [them]. (p. 62)

There is a merging of worlds and experiences that take place in that classroom space. While disciplinary instructors are the best suited to teach disciplinary writing *in situ,* they also need to be trained in how to *teach* that writing in light of the multiple worlds students bring with them to the classroom.

Despite challenges noted by other scholars regarding disciplinary faculty members' abilities to teach the discourses of their communities (National Research Council, 2000; Smit, 2004), Dr. Bianchi's own experience learning to read and write as a scientist led to her strong awareness of the needs of students coming to the discourse as newcomers (she drew on her own personal biography). As such, she developed an explicit, scaffolded approach to teaching the genres, rhetorical conventions, and critical reading strategies necessary to successfully engage with others as a scientist.

To counteract the "writing is the domain of English" perception, it is important for writing programs to work toward educating non-writing specialists about how their respective disciplines' epistemological and ideological views are reified in text and speech so that, together, these can be made transparent to newcomers. This involves disciplinary instructors becoming, if not experts, proficient in the rhetorical conventions and genres of their disciplines. Deeper scholarship into working across epistemological and ontological divides is needed, as is the preparation of junior scholars (particularly those likely to serve as supervisors) in the underpinnings of the disciplinary discourses. That way, when they are in a position of power (as a laboratory supervisor or new professor), they can adopt strategies to make disciplinary discourses accessible to as many students as possible. (A deeper discussion of these considerations is taken up in Chapter 5.)

Because mentors occupy a unique role as literacy sponsors, their being mindful of the ways in which pernicious ideologies of gratefulness, thankfulness, and preparedness are culturally shaped is critical. What may be read as a student being disinterested or underprepared might be a disconnect between two culturally shaped ways of communicating or performing. Students' performance might also be informed by how they are oriented toward the mentor and the field (e.g., being intimidated by a mentor or others within the lab, being unsure of where one fits within the space or what contributions they can make). As we educators move toward further diversifying educational and disciplinary spaces, it becomes even more salient that we stop and check ourselves and our assumptions as well as that we make sure we do not impose on students the same hardships and traumas we may have experienced ourselves.

In the next chapter, I discuss the ways in which our expectations around performativity (both physical and linguistic) can impact student success within disciplinary spaces. Through an examination of speech acts in practice, I explore how assumptions and disciplinary norms can constitute microaggressions that ultimately work toward pushing underrepresented individuals out of disciplinary spaces.

Chapter 4. Performing Race and Gender in Science

In the previous chapter, I explored how White Institutional Presence (WIP) impacts instructor ideologies and pedagogy and the impacts this has on student experiences. I also began to explore how student orientations to research spaces in the PRISM program affected engagement with texts and impacted how and what students wrote. In this chapter, I build on that work to examine performativity in greater depth by focusing the lens more specifically on linguistic and physical speech acts.

In his book *Performativity*, James Loxley (2007) summarizes Austin's seminal theory of speech acts, which highlights the ways in which what we say (our utterances) can become performative. As Loxley put it,

> Words do something in the world, something that is not just a matter of generating consequences, like persuading or amusing or alarming an audience. The promises, assertions, bets, threats and thanks that we offer one another are not this kind of action . . . .they are actions *in themselves*, actions of a distinctively linguistic kind. They are "performed," like other actions, or take place, like other worldly events, and thus make a difference in the world; it could be said that they produce a different world, even if only for a single speaker and a single addressee. (p. 2)

In other words, how we perform language and behavior and enact habits of mind mark our place in communities within a hierarchy of belonging, because to be recognized as a member of a community requires features that mark people as belonging *here* and not *there*. "Learning," Lave and Wenger (1991) wrote, "implies becoming a different person with regard to the possibilities enabled by these systems of learning" (p. 53); it "changes who we are and creates personal histories of becoming in the context of our communities" (Wenger, 1998). Speech acts function to position individuals within institutional spaces. They enact rules and norms for behavior and language, with tangible consequences for breaking those rules and norms (Butler, 1997), and create storylines (Bonilla-Silva, 2018, p. 97) that tell us who is welcome in these spaces.

I begin this chapter with a discussion of speech acts and positioning theory, drawing heavily on Austin (1975), Searle (1969), and Harré (2009), to explain how language creates and maintains institutional spaces. This includes an examination of how this process works in STEM disciplines, with an emphasis on the physical sciences. The primary focus of the chapter, however, is to illustrate what these forces look like in practice. Drawing on the experiences of the participants in this study, I show how speech acts can create an institutional space of inclusivity or can further marginalize (through microaggressions), marking individuals as members of the disciplinary community or not.

Speech Acts, Institutions, and Systems of Oppression

According to Austin (1975), every speech act has three parts: the locution (the phrase or sentence that has meaning and structure; the grammatical and syntactical elements), the illocution (the intention of the speaker), and the perlocution (the "uptake"; how the listener receives the statement; its effect on the listener). If I say the sentence, "Open the door for the dogs," the locution is the order of the words in the sentence to create meaning (stating, "Dogs door the open for," makes no grammatical sense), the illocution is my intent (I want the listener to physically open the door for the dogs), and the perlocution is how the listener hears my sentence (as a demand, as a request, as a suggestion, etc.). The speech act is successful for the speaker if the listener opens the door for the dog, regardless of how the listener feels about it.

Deeper still, Austin (1975) noted that there are multiple types of speech acts, which Searle (1969) expanded on and complicated. There are assertives (Austin called these constatives) that describe or report conditions or states of being. The statement, "There are no clouds in the sky today," constitutes an assertive. It is a statement that can be investigated and tested, proven true or false. Directives are those speech acts that command orders and make requests (i.e., the statement, "Open the door for the dogs, please.") Commissives encompass promises and the swearing to do something, as in the statement, "I promise that I will clean the kitchen tonight," (which leaves room for me to break that promise, if I so desire). Expressives articulate our feelings toward another or a situation, including congratulations and apologies. And declarations, Searle's final category, bring things into existence by the very nature of the utterance. In the context of a wedding, the statement, "I now pronounce you . . . ," by the officiant legally binds two individuals into a marriage contract. Telling a supervisor, "I quit," terminates an employer-employee relationship.

Speech act theory recognizes the role of speaker and hearer in the execution of an utterance and recognizes that each speech act comes with specific rights and duties. Who is allowed to speak and when? What authority does the speaker hold within a given context? In a marriage ceremony, the officiant holds the power to declare a marriage complete. A wedding guest, standing in the same place and uttering the same words, does not carry the power to seal the compact. Similarly, telling a stranger on the street, "I quit," in the absence of your supervisor does not mean you are now unemployed. Performative speech acts only work if the right person utters them and the right person recognizes them. (We all know there are times when we might pretend *not* to hear something, in which case we can pretend that it did not happen!) Convention, then, is important because it defines context-dependent elements—within the context of *this* space, with *these* actors, the speech act is performed successfully (even if it could be accomplished in a different way, with different actors, in a different space). As such, there are rules that govern what is allowed and not allowed within specific contexts.

Within PRISM, for example, students must follow a specific format for research proposals; a template is provided by the program with guidance on what content should be presented in each subsection of the document. A student is not allowed to submit a proposal without the sponsorship of a laboratory and the signature of their mentor, and they are expected to meet the linguistic expectations of their field (adopting the language and jargon appropriately). A failure to meet these rules means that, as we saw with Anne in Chapter 3, proposals are returned for revision and, in some cases, not funded.

In his work on positioning theory, Harré (2009) notes that the forces of speech acts and the positions the speaker and listener (and writer and reader) occupy are *themselves* embedded in storylines that are being lived by actors at any point in time. Adopting or being assigned a position in an interaction has an immediate effect on the way speech acts are interpreted and internalized. There is a difference, for example, between the sentence "Girls are terrible at science" being uttered by a casual stranger on the street and by a faculty member in a classroom because of the differences in authority that each individual holds; for the listeners, there is a difference in the perlocution (the uptake) between the students within that classroom who identify as girls and those who identify otherwise. Similarly, there is a difference between a friend reading your proposal and noting grammar issues and a faculty mentor circling all those errors in red pen. One does not have the power to fail you, while the other does, and you may feel their judgements quite differently.

The storylines individuals are raised with are assertions of possible futures. These assertions act on the world on an individual-by-individual level. If people are told throughout their entire lives—by teachers, books, public messaging—that girls do not grow up to be scientists, then these assertions create storylines by which people will view the world. These individual messages accumulate over time to regulate the parameters of an institution. In this way, speech acts present "institutional facts" (Searle, 1969) that create meaning for expected patterns of behavior and communicative norms. They create an ontology through which members of the community view the world and regulate both how the community members behave and how things are done in the community (Searle, 1969). Speech acts regulate bodies performing within the space.

It is important to pause, here, to apply a critical lens and recognize that intentionality is not a driving factor in the impact of the speech act as it is perceived by the listener. Whether someone *meant* to imply that another person did not belong, was attempting to police behavior, and so on, is irrelevant. The force on the listener—the listener's *felt experience*—is the speech act coming to fruition. These differences between how a speech act is perceived by a speaker and how it is perceived by a listener is one of the ways in which biases are enabled broadly in society. The reality of multiple perspectives contributing to interpretation can be distressing to many when discussing microaggressions (particularly related to race and gender) because it suggests that one is "damned if you do, damned if you don't." An individual may make what seems to them to be a harmless comment based on their own cultural background and experiences and, in the process, offend or harm another who does not share that same orientation. For some, such a realization could result in a throwing up of hands and a "why bother?" attitude. Recognizing that intentionality does not matter, though, can be liberating because it means that people can focus instead on the ways that social norms, disciplinary expectations, and discourses reify patriarchy, White supremacy, and classism systemically and work to do better. It provides an opportunity for people to critique and modify.

In today's U.S. society, it is widely understood that to comment on another person's physical appearance (clothing, weight, beauty, etc.) can be construed as inappropriate, depending on the context and speaker. Similarly, most understand that using racist, gendered, or ablest jokes or analogies can offend—to the degree that one may lose a job over such comments. These are not the kinds of speech-acts-as-microaggressions I examine in this chapter (though they certainly occur regularly enough in academic spaces). Instead, I look at ways behaviors, languages, social norms, and more are gendered, White-washed, and classist and how they have been institutionalized in a way that makes them hard to be seen *as* problematic unless looking at both the immediate effects of the interchange and the long term, cumulative effect of such acts.

Positioning theory recognizes the power of speech acts. In every context there are things that one is capable of doing or saying and things that one is permitted or forbidden to do. (The experiences of Anne and Madalyn in Dr. Meijer's laboratory, discussed in Chapter 3, are excellent examples of this.) These two elements of being capable and being allowed dictate what people *actually* say or do. How a speech act is understood depends on the power dynamics at play: It is an intersection of speaker, listener, and storyline because adopting or being assigned a position within an interaction has an immediate effect on the way speech acts are interpreted (United Nations University, 2015). As Butler (1997) notes, performativity "works itself out through the body: 'social conventions' can be seen as animating the bodies, which, in turn, reproduce and ritualize those conventions as practices" (p. 155). Speech acts are not simply creations in the mind of the hearer—they are actualized institutionally through vectors of oppression and privilege and have very real physical consequences (Butler, 1997; Crenshaw, 1991).

Performativity of "Scientist"

In 1975, Margaret Mead and Rhoda Métraux asked high school students in the US to draw what they saw in their mind when they heard the word "scientist." The composite result was telling:

> The scientist is a man who wears a white coat and works in a laboratory. He is elderly or middle aged and wears glasses . . . he

may wear a beard . . . he is surrounded by equipment: test tubes, Bunsen burners, flasks and bottles, a jungle gym of blown glass tubes and weird machines with dials . . . he writes neatly in black notebooks. . . . One day he may straighten up and shout: "I've found it! I've found it!" . . . Through his work people will have new and better products . . . he has to keep dangerous secrets . . . his work may be dangerous . . . he is always reading a book. (pp. 386–387)

To see if this "man of knowledge," Einstein-like stereotype persisted over time, David Wade Chambers (1983) expanded on this study to ask nearly 5,000 young children (in the second and third grades) over the course of 11 years to "draw a scientist." The results were consistent with Mead and Métraux's (1975) findings. The standard image students created included a lab coat, eyeglasses, facial growth of hair, symbols of research and knowledge (e.g., beakers, books), technology, and captions to illustrate discovery (e.g., word bubble with "Eureka!"). Only 28 of the children in Chambers' (1983) study (0.6 percent) drew a female scientist.

Since then, other researchers have replicated the "draw-a-scientist test" in various contexts. In 2018, David I. Miller and his colleagues published a meta-analysis of scholarship that had used this model to illustrate if and what had changed over time. Drawing on 78 studies (involving over 20,000 children cumulatively), their work shows that, though children's representations of "scientist" have become more gender diverse, they "still associate science with men as they grow older" (p. 1943). The meta-analysis identified that

girls on average drew 30% of scientists as male at age 6 (early elementary school . . .). However, girls switched to drawing more male than female scientists between the ages of 10 and 11 (fifth grade; end of elementary school). By age 16 (high school), girls on average drew 75% of scientists as male. In contrast, for boys, the mean percentage of male scientists changed from 83% to 98% between ages 6 and 16 . . . . (p. 1950)

Considering these representations from the perspective of speech act theory, what is the received message (perlocution) of such images? Laboratory coats, typically white, function as protection, but they also represent purity, sterility, and *objectivity*. They reinforce the ontology that anyone, at any time, can don the coat, repeat the experiment, and gain the same results, so the individual behind the work is not relevant to the knowledge discovered. Such an ontology also necessitates a lack of emotion and humanity. Eyeglasses send a message of both intelligence and intense focus. Beards are often associated with wisdom and knowledge (i.e., King Arthur's Merlin) but also rigor—as Mead and Métraux (1975) note, scientists are seen as working long and unusual hours and beards can be seen as "deviation from the accepted way of life" (p. 388). Whiteness of skin and male-ness are illustrative of authority and origins of knowledge. Taken together, this common representation of "scientist" is that of a middle-to-old-age White man with exceptional innate intelligence who works alone in the lab for long periods of time and performs secretive, complicated tasks. If we laminate onto this his use of jargon-heavy, technical language, the "scientist" becomes someone whom only an elite group of people can become.

The question that arises, then, is what happens when individuals who do not fit this mold attempt to become part of the scientific community? The simple answer is that they are positioned as deviants. Elaine Seymour and Nancy M. Hewitt (1997) demonstrated in their three-year study of women and other underrepresented groups in science that attrition from STEM disciplines is a direct result of masculine norms and values (e.g., placing students in direct competition with one another, unfriendly professors, "weed out" courses). As they explain,

> We posit that entry to freshman courses in science, mathematics or engineering suddenly makes explicit, and then heightens, what is actually a long-standing divergence in the socialization experiences of young men and women . . . of all ethnicities [who] are entering an educational system which has evolved to support the ongoing socialization of only one group—namely, white males. (pp. 258–259)

Those who persist in STEM education are considered an exception to the norm (even tokenized) and typically adopt the language and behaviors of the dominant group. Yet, even if seen as an exception, such individuals are not necessarily welcomed.

In their study of 15 women of color, Heidi B. Carlone and Angela Johnson (2007) noted that performance was a critical dimension of scientific identity: "One cannot pull off being a particular kind of person (enacting a particular identity) unless one makes visible to (*performs for*) others one's *competence* in relevant practices, and, in response, others *recognize* one's performance as credible" (p. 1190). One must do the right things, in the right ways, in the right contexts, in order to be seen by others as belonging to the group—often with a higher performance threshold for visibility. Such restraints mean that, for women and BIPOC, they cannot develop just *any* kind of scientific identity; they need to align with the "larger and more pervasive meanings of 'science people' derived from sociohistorical legacies of science" (Carlone & Johnson, 2007, p. 1192), and they must do so perfectly and exceptionally. To demonstrate anything that does not align with those sociohistorical legacies marks one as problematic and may lead to microaggressions (Pierce, 1974) from dominant groups. Many of those in their study who pushed against dominant constraints

> felt overlooked, neglected, or discriminated against by meaningful others within science . . . they felt that established

members of their science departments recognized them not as science people but, instead, as representatives of stigmatized groups. They perceived that their behaviors, or even just their appearance, triggered racial, ethnic or gender recognitions that overwhelmed their chances of being recognized as good science students. (Carlone & Johnson, 2007, p. 1202)

In what follows, I examine how performative aspects of race and gender in science disciplines impacted student participants' experiences in undergraduate research, both within PRISM as well as in external summer programs. Importantly, I will examine the ways "the subtle, mini assault" of racism and sexism (Pierce, 1974, p. 516) plays out in scientific spaces and its subsequent effect on participants' self-concept.

Microaggressions in Academic Spaces

Though John Jay and PRISM actively highlighted the multicultural nature of the institution (including publishing program documents in both English and Spanish), microaggressions that functioned on the interpersonal level still existed. The term "microaggression" was coined by Chester M. Pierce in 1974 to describe the subtle, everyday oppressions BIPOC experience and its definition has since been extended to encompass oppressions based on gender, sexual orientation, and other considerations. Important to recognize is that microaggressions are not the conscious, overt forms of racism often thought of when discussing inequity (e.g., police brutality or marching in the street with Tiki torches). Rather, microaggressions are the internalized, systemic, unconscious verbal and physical cues that tell individuals that they do not belong. Similarly, the prefix "micro" does not correlate to impact, as the felt impact of such aggressions can be enormous. Some of the myriad ways microaggressions materialize in STEM education and in other educational spaces include positive discrimination narratives, practitioner identity work (e.g., having to reaffirm expertise), the use of male pronouns or diminutives to describe scientists as a group (e.g., nerds), higher performance thresholds for visibility, tokenization, and the organization of physical spaces (e.g., the exclusion of artifacts that represent racial or gendered groups). Microaggressions erode confidence over time; they are layered assaults that accumulate and take a toll on the physiological, psychological, and academic aspects of the receiver (Pierce, 1974; Sue, 2010).

Despite John Jay's status as a HSI and MSI, many of the students in this study experienced positive discrimination narratives in the pursuit of academic and professional growth opportunities. On more than one occasion, Natalia—a high-achieving Latinx woman—wondered aloud about some of the programs, including PRISM, that focus on increasing diversity in STEM. For example, she said, "Just me being Hispanic, you know, just being a minority—I just have that intuition. Like, 'Oh, is it because I'm Hispanic [that I got this opportunity]?' So, you're thinking twice about it. And it's awful." She felt guilt at being able to apply for summer programs that friends who were not "considered a minority" were ineligible for: "Am I getting something just because I'm a minority and they want to show, like, 'Our percentages for minorities are getting higher!'" Though Natalia's academic achievements were more than enough evidence of her competence, she had internalized a feeling that her accomplishments were tainted by institutional desires to "perform" equity and inclusion.

Both John Jay and PRISM made active efforts to highlight the diversity both in the institution in general and in its STEM disciplines in particular so as to help students feel included and not tokenized. Yet, such representation does not mean that it was not sometimes seen as a marketing trope. When discussing representation, for example, Madalyn (a White woman) noted how posters hanging throughout John Jay and her department highlighted a wide variety of ethnicities and genders. "I think that the school is very enthusiastic about minority students in the sciences," she explained. She continued,

> They're the ones that get their pictures on the posters and on the website and stuff like that. The high-achieving minority students—and that's great. I feel like it's something that's coming from the administration. It's just diversity, diversity, diversity.

Though well meaning, Madalyn's description of these marketing activities revealed two things: that the experience of these promotional materials felt somewhat contrived and that she saw these individuals as exceptions (showing only the "high-achieving minority" students). Madalyn's articulation of the purpose of these promotional materials serves as an excellent example of what Sue et al. (2007) define as "microinsults," microaggressions that include "subtle snubs, frequently unknown to the perpetrator, but [that] clearly convey a hidden insulting message" (p. 274). Though Madalyn's expression of bias was unintentional, it nevertheless was there and had the potential to cause harm.

Despite John Jay's and PRISM's outward-facing marketing approaches, inclusion within laboratory spaces was not always actualized. Anne, for example, was allowed to observe in the laboratory during her first semester of undergraduate research. Her explicit role was to watch what other students were doing and help them accomplish their goals. While this role was described as part of the apprenticeship model, it nevertheless conveyed to Anne, an anxious, young Black woman, that she was not capable or trustworthy enough to engage in even the most entry-level research activities—particularly because other students (like Madalyn) who entered PRISM in the same cohort and who joined the same laboratory were given far more responsibility and autonomy. Though Anne made formal appointments with her mentor to discuss next steps on creating her own research project, as Anne put it, "every time I would make an appointment, something would come up and the appointment would get [canceled]." Anne often described tasks her mentor gave her as things "to keep me busy" rather than as things to help her learn. Even when her own research began, Anne found herself frequently being taken off her project to work on other people's research. Cumulatively, these experiences in the first year of undergraduate research conveyed to Anne that her value in the laboratory was considerably less than others'. Her value was in helping others accomplish their goals, not in pursuing goals of her own.

Amrita's first experience in undergraduate research was similar. Prior to joining Dr. Bianchi's laboratory, she was in another that was heavily chemistry-based, and her faculty mentor at that time was what might best be described as *aloof*. As Amrita explained, "I felt like she didn't really mentor us very much. It was much more of like . . . she told us what she wanted you to accomplish, and you just had to figure out how to do that." It was an experience similar to Anne's. Each week, Amrita showed up at a prescribed time on a prescribed day and completed the prescribed tasks, nothing more or less, as though a cog in a larger machine. Though Amrita was an active member of the research team, when it came time to write the results in a paper and submit it for publication, she was not part of that process. Though she never stated so explicitly, the fact that Amrita chose to leave that initial experience and seek out a new mentor who would "walk [her] through the steps" and actually guide her in the process of conducting research spoke to the kind of scientist she was developing an affinity for.

These two laboratory experiences represent what is often justified as simply the way in which science works—the apprenticeship model described by Lave and Wenger (1991). In this model, students enter a space as novices. Through time and exposure, they pick up the procedural knowledge, discourse conventions, and habits of mind embedded in the disciplinary space and, ultimately, move toward becoming experts in the field. Yet, how this apprenticeship experience is enacted has significant consequences on the student. Natalia, Ruben, and (eventually) Amrita had very different experiences than those described by the traditional apprenticeship model precisely because of the orientation to science that their mentors held.

When Natalia met with her mentor, Dr. Bianchi, to discuss working with her in undergraduate research, Natalia described Dr. Bianchi as "so willing to tell me about the projects and what's going on." The interaction she described was one full of both enthusiasm and transparency. Dr. Bianchi made clear to Natalia that this was a hands-on learning process and that she was not expected to know much as she entered the experience but that she would be provided all of the tools and resources she would need to be successful. These included pairing Natalia with a peer mentor, providing a variety of resources on the research that was taking place in the laboratory already, meeting with her regularly to discuss readings and procedures, and working side-by-side in the lab to show Natalia what the techniques she read about looked like in practice. Natalia was engaged in her own research activities from the start, helping her to build confidence and autonomy as a researcher. Amrita experienced the same incorporation into the laboratory when she left her first URE and started working with Dr. Bianchi. One critical aspect of both women's experience was that issues of gender equity in science were never hidden, which was important for Natalia given her early orientation to race and gender inequity in STEM disciplines in high school. Toward the later period of both women's UREs, Dr. Bianchi became pregnant, and she modeled positively what balancing family and a career in science could look like.

Though both Natalia and Amrita understood the rigor that scientific research entails, it was eye-opening for each of them to see how an established female scientist could juggle the demands of pregnancy and family life with the work of the laboratory. For Natalia, this was a critical experience. She and her fiancé had begun talking about their future plans and their mutual desire to have a large family. Doubt as to whether she could be both an attentive mother and a scientist had crept into Natalia's mind over time, and she worried that the two were mutually exclusive. Seeing someone she respected model the balance showed her a possible future for herself. Because this balance was sometimes messy, Natalia was also reminded that science is a human endeavor and that humans are not always perfect.

Ruben's experience was similar to Natalia's and Amrita's. His mentor, Dr. Martinez, created a scaffolded entry into the URE that allowed Ruben to be involved from the very beginning. She provided readings, met regularly to speak with him about the texts, offered guidelines for note-taking, and gave hands-on instruction within the laboratory. Importantly, as a native Spanish speaker, she and Ruben conversed regularly in both Spanish and English. The language affinity he shared with his mentor was important to Ruben when he joined Dr. Martinez's laboratory because it was a point of connection. Even though their ethnicities were different, they shared a language. In both laboratories, students were made to feel welcome. The masculinized, competitive nature of science was set to the side in favor of helping students feel welcome and capable. Students in these spaces were acculturating to science, not assimilating—both their home cultures and lived experiences *and* the culture of science were embraced.

From Inside to Outside the College

In addition to engaging in undergraduate research at John Jay, many students in PRISM are encouraged during the summer months to pursue internships and other research opportunities outside the institution. Such additional experiences can build exposure to the field while also making students more competitive for graduate programs and employment opportunities. As a result of feeling marginalized within her URE, Anne opted to seek external opportunities to build her resume and research experience during both the academic year and the summer months. In addition to working alongside a fetal pathologist who helped her feel more competent as a scientist (for a detailed description, see Falconer, 2019a), she pursued summer research opportunities at a variety of institutions.

In the spring before her final year, Anne was accepted into a summer URE at a prestigious college of medicine in the city. Of the 50 students participating in the program, though, only four of them (including Anne) were Black, which led to her feeling tokenized in a direct way. All of the Black students were women, and the three living on campus were housed separately from the other students in a different building. When I asked if anyone commented on this, Anne laughed and said, "I was like, hmmm . . . I think they planned this." Anne decided she would not complain because the arrangements afforded the women more breathing room—but the physical isolation marked them as "special." They were admitted into the program but physically separated from the other 46 participants. In their more intimate, private space away from the other students, Anne and her peers were able to speak about their experiences in the summer program candidly. Her roommate was paired in the laboratory with an Indian male doctoral student that seemed to undermine the woman's success at every turn. "He gave her contaminated cells," Anne remarked,

> and he was so rude to her. He wouldn't communicate. . . . My friend said (she was Jamaican) . . . , she was like, "The only thing stopping me from cursing him was the fact that if I curse him they're gonna be like, "That black girl." She said, she was talking to me, she literally cried. She cried. How terrible he was. I was like, if it was me, I probably would've quit or I would've complained a long time ago.

Anne was fortunate, unlike her roommate, in that she was paired with two female researchers who were supportive and understanding. On her first day, she was introduced to a variety of research projects and given a week to select the one in which she was most interested. By default, her selection of a project paired her with the doctoral student who would serve as her mentor. Anne described her immediate affinity with this researcher, Mary, in positive terms ("friendly," "sweet," "engaging") and spoke of her introduction to the laboratory as "welcoming" and "open." By creating an inclusive space where Anne was able to choose a project that seemed interesting to her and by making clear that Anne was both welcome in the lab and belonged in the space, Mary fostered an environment that meant Anne felt comfortable owning her agency.

In her first visit to Mary's lab, Anne noticed a sticky note on the computer that simply said, "Do complement." When Anne asked what that meant, Mary explained that it was a procedural step in the research on herpes simplex virus that she had been meaning to do for the past year but had yet to complete. Because she felt "attached" to Mary already, Anne responded, "Well, while *I'm* here, why don't we work on it? Cause I can do it, and you'll actually have the [results]." In that brief moment, Anne's summer research project was born.

Over lunch later in the summer, I asked Anne to explain what "complement" means and was struck by the ease and sophistication of her explanation in comparison to projects she had done with both Dr. Meijer and Dr. Brennan (the fetal pathologist):

> The complement protein system—it's the way our immune system fights against bacteria. So, there's like neutralization, where the antibodies surround the virus preventing it from entering the host. There is ADCC—antibody-dependent cell cytotoxicity. So, that's basically when the antibody binds to the virus, and the antibody also binds to the host cell, and then the virus dies. But neutralization, with most vaccines, you know like before they used to put an attenuated strain of the virus inside you to create the vaccine? They are trying to move away from that because, basically, you don't want to infect the person. So then they came up with viral proteins—the proteins *of* the virus creates the same response. . . . So complement—they have three systems. The alternative pathway, the classical pathway, and the lectin pathway. The classical pathway is antibody-dependent, so [Mary] wanted me to see if that was another method that [the vaccine] could work by.

Anne's discussion of the research and mechanisms involved continued on for some time, with the disciplinary jargon rolling off her tongue with ease. I noticed, too, that her posture was different. She held herself taller, seemed more poised, and did not casually insert self-deprecating remarks about her skills as a scientist as she had in earlier interviews. Her confidence had risen enormously in this brief period of time.

Describing the experience with Mary as a mentor, Anne said, "She was *very* patient with me." First, Mary asked Anne to write her own protocol, including the Methods section. Though Mary already had a protocol in place, she wanted Anne to have the experience of writing one from scratch. When Anne was done, Mary reviewed it. "I got one section completely right," Anne laughed; "all of the others—they weren't wrong, but they were vague." Mary discussed with Anne the places where more specificity was needed and offered guidance in revision (suggesting alternative language, for example). Through this experience, Anne learned a valuable lesson: "When you are writing protocols, even a person who doesn't know what to do should be able to repeat it. So you have to put in how much of this, how much of that—stuff I didn't know."

Mary went out of her way to walk Anne through the protocol, step by step—first having Anne watch, then letting Anne do the protocol while Mary watched, and then leaving Anne to work on her own (encouraging Anne's feeling of competence). She provided Anne with her own vial of cells that she was responsible for caring for and growing over the summer: "She showed me what [the healthy cells] looked like, she showed me what they look like when they're infected. . . . And everybody was so nice to me."

During her eight weeks in the program, Anne was able to contribute significantly to Mary's project. By "doing complement," the team discovered that the classical pathway was involved in killing virally infected cells just as effectively as neutralization, providing insight into alternative vaccines—ones that remove the virus through modification of the viral membrane glycoproteins. Anne was required to present this knowledge in a poster session at the end of the program. She wrote and designed the poster entirely on her own, with minimal feedback from Mary or Mary's principal investigator. An excerpt of this poster is provided in Figure 4.1. In this excerpt, which is representative of the poster as a whole, it is clear that Anne had begun to understand the ways in which the presentation of scientific research in a poster is a balancing act between maintaining credibility as a scientist and being understood by laypeople. She immediately introduced the significance of the research, both on an individual and global level (how the virus presents in human bodies versus the prevalence of the virus internationally). The introduction continued with more specificity about the project itself and the mechanisms Anne's work investigated. Throughout, she fluidly balanced disciplinary jargon with explanations of how the mechanisms worked, ensuring that her varied audience would at the very least understand the gist of the work if not the work in depth.

A second interesting element of the poster was Anne's decision to present the Methods section as a visual, rather than as the typical numbered list. Figure 4.2 shows the sequence of steps in a diagram that Anne included in the poster. Again, Anne met multiple audiences while still addressing the rhetorical situation effectively. Short descriptions of each step were included beneath each phase of the protocol, succinctly describing what took place, and her careful use of directional arrows and simple imagery helped the reader *see* how the complement serum affected viral cells.

When speaking about her experience with the poster—both constructing the document on her own as well as presenting the research in a conference format—Anne was confident and proud. "I didn't have to do a lot of practicing," she explained about preparing for the poster session; "I *knew* the research and I understood it." It was clear that this was Anne's work and that she *owned* it—she embodied the role of scientific researcher with ease. Anne noted that PRISM's program coordinator wanted her to attend the Annual Biomedical Research Conference for Minority Students (ABRCMS; now the Annual Biomedical Research Conference for Minoritized Scientists) in the coming fall. When I asked if she wanted to attend, Anne explained that she was very interested in doing so, but that the only way she would go would be if she could present her summer research.[8] She had no interest in presenting the poster she had done for Dr. Meijer's laboratory because she was embarrassed about how little she had contributed to that project.

---

8. Anne submitted her summer research abstract to ABRCMS for consideration and was accepted to present her poster at that year's conference.

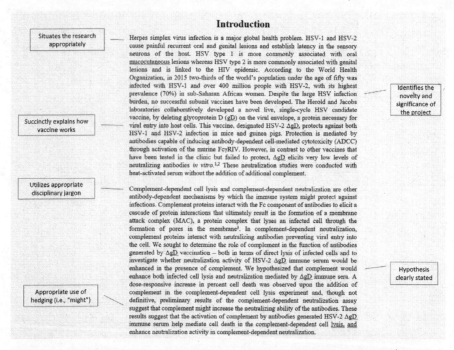

Figure 4.1. The introductory section to Anne's summer research poster. This poster was written exclusively by Anne with minimal edits from her mentor, Mary.

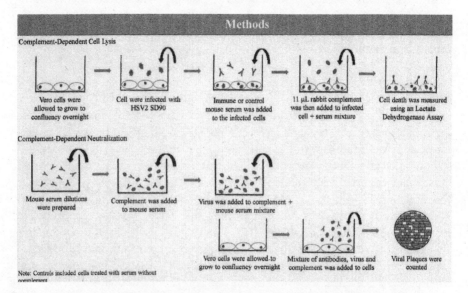

Figure 4.2. The method section of Anne's poster. This section was constructed as a visual, rather than as a textual list, which assisted readers in quickly understanding the protocol Anne followed in the project.

When I asked if she planned to continue with Meijer in the fall, Anne was sheepish. "I don't know," she mumbled. "I feel bad if I just leave her. Will she feel like she's a bad teacher? I don't want that on my conscience." After having had experiences elsewhere to compare to, Anne explained, "I need someone— I don't need someone to *push* me, but I can't do everything by myself." She was realizing that she benefited when given initial guidance on new procedures and then given room to explore them on her own (as Mary had provided). She did not want to have to chase after someone for information or supplies or feel like a scheduled meeting would be canceled at the last minute (or forgotten entirely, which had happened with Dr. Meijer enough times to make Anne cautious). "If I have a question, I'm not scared to ask—but [Dr. Meijer] won't reply for two weeks and by then I've forgotten what I asked," and because of this, she found, the work moved in fits and starts and increased her frustration and her feeling of incompetence.

Two poignant moments stand out as representative of how strong mentor fit contributed to Anne's development and performance as a scientist. After completing her research for Mary and presenting at the poster session, Anne's understanding of the work she had done was complemented by Mary, who Anne reported said, "We were watching you speak and you were so fluid. You *know* the research." And then later, Anne reported, while Anne was eating cake that Mary had made as part of a send-off party, Mary said, "How does it feel to be a scientist?" The second moment occurred in November of that same year. After successfully presenting her summer research at ABRCMS, Anne left the conference as the holder of the Best Poster Award. She had finally reached a stage where she not only felt like a scientist but was being recognized as such from others within the scientific community.

Self-Efficacy, Social Factors, and Persistence

People's levels of self-efficacy, as Albert Bandura (1997) defined and described, are reflections of how much they believe in their own ability to control their motivation, behavior, and social environment. How people see themselves—how they *position* themselves—and the storylines they believe influence the ways in which they experience given moments and contexts and are predictors of how much energy they might be willing to expend to reach their goals. In the US, the "build-yourself-up-from-the-bootstraps" storyline has effectively ingrained institutions with White meritocratic discourse. If people work hard enough, *if* they put the time and labor in, *then* their just rewards will come. This discourse, however, makes invisible systemic barriers related to class, gender, and race. For example, practices such as school districting and the funding of public schools, which make funds available based on the district's socioeconomic resources (e.g., taxes), disproportionately affect BIPOC communities and have impacts on school resources, public services, and more.

When examining the impacts of race and gender performativity in institutional spaces, it is challenging to parse where learning disruptions occur because of racism, because of sexism, because of classism, or because of something entirely different. Yet, it is precisely this invisibility and elusiveness that allows systemic inequalities to persist and why taking an intersectional approach is important to the dismantling of these oppressions. In most instances, vectors of oppression rarely operate in isolation; they intersect to create added layers of oppression onto some individuals and mask oppression for others. For example, because socio-economic class and race are so intricately tied in the US, when educational inequity is noticed along racial lines, it is explained away as something else because low-income White people experience similar challenges.

These oppressions are hidden when students enter college classrooms. Educators do not know what the students' educational backgrounds are; they can only know that the students performed well enough to arrive in the educators' spaces. Thus, the narrative of "grit" continues, assuming everyone to be on a level playing field—as the story goes, if you show up and put the time in, you will succeed. However, individuals' understanding of cultural norms and expectations strongly influences how they interact with others and build personal and professional connections, and their self-efficacy within specific contexts (i.e., science) can also impact their persistence and retention despite academic performance. Kyle M. Whitcomb and coauthors (2020) noted in their study of engineering students that self-efficacy was not necessarily correlated with grades—women often reported having lower levels of self-efficacy despite high performance. Doing well in a discipline does not necessarily correlate with feeling like a member of the discipline. Drawing on self-reported data, in this section I expand on that discussion to incorporate self-efficacy, showing how it intersected with social factors and influenced engagement with scientific discourse.

As discussed in Chapter 2, Ruben chose to pursue a science-related career based partly on altruistic reasons—he wanted to "be useful"—and partly because he saw the field as ripe with economic and personal opportunity. Similarly, he enrolled in PRISM because he saw it as helping him reach his end goals of acquiring a master's degree and finding solid employment. Despite these ambitions, Ruben had doubts about his ability to do the transactional and discursive work of the laboratory. He reported that he "was afraid at the beginning" because he was intimidated by math and science at the advanced level. In reading scientific articles for his first review of the literature, he noted that "the words and the instruments are challenging," that his notebook was "a mess," and that he felt like "a beginner scientist." This sense of self at the start of undergraduate research is not uncommon and not noteworthy in itself. Almost all students in this study reported being nervous as they approached the research aspect of their discipline for the first time. What is worth paying attention to is if and how Ruben's sense of self changed with exposure over time, what factors played roles in any change, and whether there were similar trajectories within the reading and writing practices of the lab.

As Ruben engaged in undergraduate research (typically five hours per week), he interacted not only with his mentor but also with other student researchers in the laboratory. From these peers, he learned how to organize his notebook so that "everything is in order and [it follows] the steps of the procedure that we're doing." In his reading practices, though, he struggled in that first year to make sense of the texts, often getting lost in terminology and methods. Like many students engaging with difficult texts for the first time, he grabbed onto the parts that made sense to him—mostly descriptions of methods that were familiar from lab work—and glossed over the rest. It became clear in my discussions with his mentor about this early period of time that coursework had not prepared Ruben for the ways in which scientists find and mentally engage with knowledge. Though his mentor noted repeatedly in our discussions that so much of scientific research is *reading,* Ruben had not quite grasped this after the first year. "He had no idea," his mentor explained, describing his unfamiliarity with the search engine PubMed or how to find and read relevant academic articles.

I have written elsewhere in detail about the impact of this mentoring relationship on Ruben's scientific writing (Falconer, 2019b) as well as about how faculty and family expectations effected Ruben's discursive development (Falconer, in press). What I wish to focus on here is not how Ruben's mentor guided him through his reading and writing practices but on his self-efficacy as a scientist and how that impacted his performativity as an undergraduate researcher and his engagement with scientific writing. Despite starting undergraduate research with enthusiasm, Ruben's engagement with the laboratory work slowly and steadily faded over the course of the three academic years covered in this study. This was in part because of the multiple demands placed on him from within and outside of John Jay (family, work, coursework, etc.), partly to unforeseen hurdles, and partly because the pace of research was much slower than he had expected.

In our first discussion, Ruben talked excitedly about how, if his research project worked, he and his mentor would write and submit a journal article about the project (three months later). That did not happen; in fact, the work took longer than expected and had a change in trajectory partway through. The research in the lab shifted toward an extraction method that another student had developed. At the end of the first complete year of research, Ruben's energy level had dropped considerably. When I asked how he juggled all of the different commitments, he let out an audible sigh and said, "Yeah, I mean—I just have to do it. It's hard, but it's okay. I've survived so far, so I can't just quit now." In reflecting on his academic progress, Ruben was proud of himself, noting how his hard work, "hours of studying and studying, practice and practice" had helped him achieve things he previously thought he would "never be able" to do. But his enthusiasm for his research and schooling was very low, and he declared himself still "a beginner scientist."

When discussing WIP, racism, sexism, etc., it is easy to default to discussions of harm or inequality as the result of overt bias (the lead scientist who claims that all women cry in his lab, for example, or the instructor who asks the only Black or Latinx student in the class to discuss their experience with race). What Ruben's experience helps us bring to light are the ways in which WIP can impact students so subtly that it looks like something other than what it is. Like slowly chipping away at a stone, the small disruptions, personal expense, and extra labor that Ruben experienced on his journey began to wear him down. Though he could mark the ways in which he was growing as a scientist and as a scientific writer, his momentum was slowing and, with it, his commitment to and engagement with the discipline. By the middle of his second year in undergraduate research, Ruben was already discussing how, after he graduated, he would take time away from school and work in construction to earn "some decent pay." When asked if he would consider a degree beyond the master's, he replied with an emphatic, "No! I'm already too old for a PhD. I can't any more." He simply wanted to finish, work in "a clean setting," and earn a decent wage. Compounding this situation was the reality that Ruben's immigration status was in flux. A DREAMer[9], he came to the US at the age of ten and, *18 years later*, he was still trying to finalize his citizenship status. "That's one of the things that is holding me down, you know?" he explained. "It's part of it, you know, because at the same time this thing has motivated me to get an education and be useful to society. But I'm not a US citizen and this puts a halt on my movement."

About this time, Ruben's mentor had also noticed a significant "attitude shift" that was concerning her. He had seemingly disengaged from the laboratory, missing meetings, not showing up during the week, and being mentally absent. His discursive work was also showing a lack of commitment—by her account, he seemed not to be reading as much and not retaining as much of what he read. This is not to say that his awareness of the skills needed to conduct research had faded away, only that he seemed to be taking the path of least resistance toward completion. After some probing about why he was seemingly less engaged, Ruben disclosed to me that he found out he needed to take one class more than he thought he needed to meet graduation requirements, which meant an additional semester that he had to pay for out of pocket. He also had started to look at job opportunities and was feeling disheartened. His goal was to work in a toxicology laboratory, but after reviewing job announcements and talking with hiring managers, he learned that, in New York State, an additional "medical laboratory license" was required, a license that a BS in forensic science did not qualify him for. By his description, this license required an entirely separate degree that entailed at least 15 months of full-time academic work and research. Though he did have an academic advisor, that person seemed to have

---

9.   The Development, Relief, and Education for Alien Minors Act, known as the DREAM Act, provides temporary residency for minors who are illegal immigrants in the United States. If the individuals meet certain qualifications later, they can apply for permanent residency.

missed the fact that Ruben's schedule and the degree requirements were not aligned as well as the fact that the degree would not help him achieve the goals he set out for himself. Combined with the questioning of allegiances he received from work colleagues and family, Ruben felt defeated.

The White meritocratic storyline that Ruben had entered his academic career with—that if you work hard enough, you can achieve anything and that race and economic background did not matter if you cared enough—ran headlong into a different storyline. Working hard can only get you so far. Without guidance along the way to help you chart your course and navigate obstacles, you can quickly find yourself in lands you had not planned on visiting. Without financial and academic support, the exhaustion of tightened budgets and extra labor can induce a level of exhaustion that is hard to overcome on your own and can sap energy away from learning new things. And these hurdles—this exhaustion and frustration, this extra labor that disproportionately effects underrepresented minorities in STEM education—can cause you to withdraw, to pull away from the very thing you intended to do.

Conversely, when students have a reprieve from these outside burdens, there are opportunities to thrive. Amrita's second proposal was simply a resubmission of her first without edits or addendum. This allowed her to continue her research into the summer. A more significant third proposal came in the fall of 2016, after she spent the first part of the summer completing her data collection on her first project and then participating in a study abroad experience with a nongovernmental organization. When we spoke after her trip, she was in the process of putting together her data so that she could run statistical tests and then begin writing a paper, with the hopes of submitting for publication by spring. At the time of our interview, Amrita was not sure what her fall project would actually be, only that Dr. Bianchi had offered her a place as part of a team on a more substantial endeavor that would require a little less of her time. Though she had submitted an abstract to a conference during the late spring (and had been accepted), various extenuating circumstances had prevented her team from attending. However, she had submitted the same abstract to another professional conference and had been accepted there as well, suggesting that her abstract had successfully employed the conventions of scientific discourse. Because she was still in the process of analyzing her data, Amrita had not yet begun thinking about her conference presentation (which was just over a month away).

I was curious whether, after having so much success and time to work on her own research project in the lab, Amrita was headed into her second research year and first professional conference feeling like a scientist. She replied,

> Um, I think I didn't for a long time because I often—I think for
> a while now my trajectory has sort of been to become a doctor.
> But, because both of my parents are doctors, I always rejected
> the idea of becoming a doctor. . . . I tried to pick every other

possible career for myself besides being a doctor and so I think for a while I knew that I liked science and I knew I was really good at it, but I almost rejected it because I was like "I don't want to have anything to do with that." But I think now that I have sort of overcome that stupid idea and so [have] actually accepted the fact that that's something that I really want to do. It wasn't just that my parents were doctors that I rejected the idea. For me it was, again—it's this idea of *knowing*. . . . I needed to come up with a reason myself besides, like, "Oh, my parents are doctors, I'll become a doctor, too." And then once I came up with that reason for myself and I realized that a doctor is what I want to do, I think then again that identity comes with that.

Much of this identity clarification came from the extracurricular activities Amrita was involved in—internships with hospitals and public health nongovernmental organizations—as well as opportunities in the laboratory. During the early summer and into the fall, she not only conducted research, she also mentored incoming undergraduate research students, helping her to see that she enjoyed teaching as an aspect of science. This identity clarification caused her to change her major from forensic science to cell and molecular biology so that she could avoid taking the extra courses required of forensic science majors that would be of no help for medical school.

During those first few weeks of the fall semester, Amrita was busy wrapping up her data analysis from her first project, taking classes, and simultaneously doing an internship with a local hospital while trying to work with her new project team to work out the details of the trials. As she put it, "I feel like I waited until the last minute to do it because I was just like, 'I don't know what to write.'" Despite having meetings with the team about the project (which was focused on identifying chemical cues used in insect reproduction), her experience was that the writing "was a lot more *vague*." The specificity of her first proposal was such that she "knew exactly what [she] was doing [and] could take that proposal and *use it* to conduct that experiment again." But the second project turned out to be much more about the "big picture ideas of what [the team was] doing and leaving out the specifics, because [they] didn't really know what the specifics *were*"—a reality that is far more common in the work of professional scientists. Despite the imputed vagueness, Amrita's second proposal was much more succinct, and the feedback from Dr. Bianchi was closer to the later drafts of her first proposal than the earlier; Amrita was successfully engaging with the genre of the proposal on this second major attempt, and the amount of editing by her mentor was noticeably low. Most of the mentor comments and edits focused on areas where Amrita could add some content and additional citations (e.g., "Put in a statement about the importance of visual cues"; "There are some studies on [cues] to cite in your intro"). The Materials and Methods section was virtually untouched and, following the program coordinator's suggestion on the first proposal, the appendixes included appropriate visuals to offer evidence for claims Amrita made. Rather than five drafts, this time around there were only three, with only minor edits between each.

The biggest challenge Amrita noted with this second proposal had to do with citations—in particular, finding appropriate sources to use. As she remarked, "I think [our field] is such a small— Like it's a very specific field and it's hard to find good sources if you're not already familiar with the key players in the field." Because Dr. Bianchi both highlighted areas where additional citations were needed *and* provided some guidance on who to cite, Amrita was then able both to build her understanding of the appropriate way to cite evidence as well as get a sense of which scientific authors are considered credible. Amrita's second proposal was accepted without changes, and this time she did not receive any feedback from the program coordinator (which is largely understood to be a positive sign for continuing research students).

Two important changes during this second year occurred that influenced Amrita's professional identity development, which in turn had effects on her discursive identity. The first was that she took on a significant mentoring and management role for the lab, ensuring that the seven new lab members were properly oriented and trained on the equipment. This positioned Amrita as a leader and less of a newcomer than the other students and solidified her affinity for teaching. It also put her in a position where she had to translate complicated techniques and jargon into language newcomers would understand. The second change was that the new project involved working in partnership with a doctoral student and a faculty member at a separate institution. Though Amrita was still under the supervision of Dr. Bianchi and had a partner in her laboratory work (another undergraduate student), Dr. Bianchi gave the two of them space to conduct their half of the research without looking over their shoulders. Though not explicitly stated, this freedom positioned Amrita as a scientist at a level higher than is typically thought of for undergraduates.

This last element became important when, in the fall semester, it became clear that something in the preliminary trial protocol was not working as it should have theoretically. Despite the fact that the protocol was failing, the team continued to try the same approach over and over and over again. For Amrita, this was frustrating. "It's not exactly how I would describe 'good science' work," she explained. She continued,

> I think sometimes when you want something to work—like, you know theoretically it *should* work, but something is not working, you *look* for it to work. . . . If I have to look at what we've been doing so far, I would say *this* is not working. . . . It could work, but we have to make some sort of change.

And make a change is what she did. As she and her partner conducted yet another preliminary trial according to the protocol, they began to talk. In addition to realizing that they had to overtly tell the team that they were spinning their wheels, Amrita and her partner began to assess. They went "back to square one" and tried to work out where the trial was going astray:

> So we set up our own trials and things like that, that was kind of separate from what they had been doing this entire time, and we were able to run some things, which gave us some clarity on what's going on. And that was really exciting, 'cause it was like, you know this has been such a mess the entire time, and like it was good to finally take a step back and kind of go back to the basics.

Amrita and her partner took their insights, refined written protocol, and detailed notes with results to Dr. Bianchi, who was incredibly impressed. When Amrita and I spoke, Dr. Bianchi was at the partner institution presenting the materials to the other half of the team. Amrita's professional scientific identity seemed at this point to be getting stronger in that she did not question whether she was allowed to pursue this alternative line of inquiry; she just did it, trusting the knowledge that she had acquired over time, and it paid off. She also demonstrated an understanding of the importance of *documenting* her knowledge in a way that the other team members would be receptive to and understand. This experience solidified for her one aspect of being a "good" scientist: "I think the biggest thing is to not get up on the fact that you think you're supposed to be right."

Amrita's feelings about scientific writing had also shifted over time, and they were influenced not only by the laboratory but also by her writing-intensive biochemistry course (taught by another faculty mentor who embraced explicit instruction). This course required full-length laboratory reports each week, and though there was no variability in the genre requirements, the reports reinforced for Amrita that there were commonalities *across* genres:

> I think scientific writing is interesting in that there's almost a template that you follow. It's not like normal writing. You know, like A, B, C, D, E, F, G needs to go in your Introduction. Right? It's not like you can just write whatever you want. . . . You have key things you need to include that can be generalized over any sort of experiment, over any sort of scientific discipline.

This "generic template" idea was strengthened by her belief that there really was no room for creativity in scientific writing: "The purpose of the paper is to say what you did, it's to describe the research. And I think putting creativity in sort of distracts from that purpose." So while she was becoming more facile with scientific discourse and genres, Amrita had not yet grown to a point where she could see the rhetorical, suasive aspects involved. Scientific writing had more to do with documenting data and reporting information in the IMRaD format than anything else.

This thinking carried through to the presentation Amrita gave at an important professional conference during that semester. After analyzing a considerable amount of data from her first project, Amrita put together a PowerPoint presentation of her results. In her preparation, rhetorical situation became salient:

> I think the proposal needed to be detailed and needed to be what you're doing and why you're doing it. Whereas, I think that in the actual presentation, it was a lot of explaining the use of forensic entomology and then narrowing down to my research in particular, how that contributes to the field, and *then* actually describing my research.

Her presentation followed the conventions of IMRaD; however, she implemented that format for a much broader audience than she usually wrote for—forensic scientists in general. In the first draft of the presentation, Amrita opened with an orientation to her sub-discipline, situating its place in forensic science as a whole and explaining the use of the specific organism used in estimating post-mortem interval. This was an important rhetorical move because the sub-discipline is relatively new (approximately 40 years old) and is greeted with suspect by the multiple disciplinary communities it straddles. Amrita also included in her introduction information about variables that affect organism behavior, which is a critical factor in the research she was conducting. She followed this introduction with a discussion of the materials and methodology used, which incorporated appropriate specifics, such as species and trademark names, as well as the research protocol. Finally, she focused the bulk of the presentation on results, utilizing a series of graphs, diagrams, and photographs, wrapping up with a bullet-point list of conclusions.

The feedback Dr. Bianchi offered during the composing of the presentation was largely focused on images—the inclusion of specific images ("Put some images here, images break up your slide and keep the audience's interest. Just be sure to cite the images if you take from image searches . . . "; "Put a picture here of your set up if you have any")—as well as formatting ("Try to put the y axis to only one decimal"; "Format this graph like the previous one"). Later drafts of the PowerPoint presentation focused not on the slides themselves but also on the points Amrita should be sure to talk about—the organization of the oral aspect of the presentation. Interestingly, both Amrita and Dr. Bianchi opted for an extemporaneous approach to the presentation rather than preparing a script in advance. In this way, they both seemed to privilege the data on the slides over the words Amrita would use to present them.

Considerations and Applications

Systems of oppression—patriarchy, White supremacy, classism—become invisible and evasive in their institutionalization, which allows them to persist. Because of this invisibility and evasiveness, it becomes easy for minoritized individuals to internalize barriers to success as the result of deficits within themselves: If the system tells me that I do not belong, if I cannot successfully navigate the labyrinth, then I must not belong here. Yet, it is the systems themselves that are problematic and require closer critique.

In this chapter, I have examined the ways in which the URE participants embodied speech acts through performativity. I have shown how small acts of indifference and "the way we do things in science" can manifest as microaggressions that make minoritized individuals feel unwelcome. Anne's experience illustrates the importance of meeting students where they are and of recognizing the value their diverse experiences bring to our educational spaces, even when gaps persist. Ruben's case highlights how an individual is likely to not engage with or learn a new discourse if they do not see it as being part of themselves or as something that aligns with their future. Amrita's story shows us how students can flourish when they adopt the disciplinary community as their own and have the resources and support to pursue their research without added burdens.

As faculty members working with women and BIPOC students in STEM disciplines, it is critical that we unpack what it means to successfully perform as a member of the discipline in both behavior and discourse. Quite often, as faculty members we uphold structures and policies that have been handed down to us without actively asking why they exist, who they serve, and whether they are truly necessary for the advancement of our disciplinary work. One direct, actionable way of enacting such questioning is to adapt the antiracist writing assessment framework that Inoue and Poe (2020) offer so that we ask similar questions of our disciplines and educational spaces:

- What do we think constitutes a "good scientist"? What does a good scientist look like? Why does a good scientist look like that? Is there space for difference?
- What are your goals for the students participating in your classroom or laboratory? Are they reasonable? Do they account for the extra labor and additional responsibilities students may have to juggle?
- How do the ways in which you interact with and assess those students reflect your goals? Are those practices equitable? Are they causing microaggressions?
- How do the backgrounds and experiences of students in your classroom or laboratory differ from your own? Are you making unfair assumptions about them?

- How are you positioning students within your classroom or laboratory space? What messaging are you providing about whether or not they belong?
- What are the power dynamics of the space? How are you including students as knowledge-makers and individuals with power?
- Who is represented in your learning space? Who is visible in texts, theory, and physical representations?
- What products do you expect your students to be able to produce? At what level?

To counteract the daily microaggressions students may experience, it is critical that faculty members offer *microinclusions*: moments that tell students that they *do* belong, that their perspectives and cultures and discourses have an important place within disciplinary spaces. But that work cannot be successfully done without active reflection and conscious, authentic moves to recognize difference as a value-added component to educational spaces. To be inclusive and accountable, faculty members need to confront the frictions that cause resistance to change—whether the frictions be psychological, physical, or ontological.

At the beginning of Chapter 3, I introduced the idea that undergraduate research experiences serve as a "third space" where students' home discourses and sociocultural orientations and those of the mentors' come in contact with one another in important ways. In the next chapter, I examine the ways in which inclusive program structure and pedagogy was enacted within some PRISM spaces to move toward counterspaces. While the program and mentors consistently enacted some disciplinary ways of being and knowing that reinforced systemic bias, they also made moves to disrupt inequity in other ways, creating spaces where mentors and students could safely critique problematic aspects of STEM education.

Chapter 5. Structuring Communities of Understanding and Support

In the preceding chapters, I introduced the idea that undergraduate research experiences serve as a "third space" (Bhabha, 1994; Gutiérrez et al., 1999; Soja, 1996; Moje, et al., 2004)—a space where "different instructional, home, and community knowledge bases and Discourses" (Moje, et al., 2004, p. 41) come in contact with one another in important ways. I also explored the way these spaces can demand certain performances by minoritized individuals within them and the social and emotional implications of such performativity. Here, I will expand on the small and large acts of resistance to these challenges that occurred in PRISM at both an individual and institutional level, illustrating the ways in which a third space can contribute to building a *counterspace*—a safe space of negotiation, initiation, inclusion, and critique.

More than simply "safe social spaces," (Ong et al., 2018, p. 207), counterspaces are intentional settings that allow for adaptive responding, spaces where marginalized individuals can "maintain psychological well-being despite oppressive conditions" through employment of coping, resilience, and resistance (Case and Hunter, 2012, p. 259). Counterspaces may take varied forms, from formalized initiatives to individual relationships that are explicitly cultivated, but all allow lived experience to be acknowledged and validated. Adaptive responding, as Case and Hunter (2012) explain, can be enacted through narrative identity work (e.g., resisting traditional storylines related to race, gender, or discipline), acts of resistance (e.g., challenging traditional norms), and direct relational transactions (e.g., the relationships between individuals that foster security and autonomy), all of which are discussed in this chapter. Though PRISM does not explicitly name itself as a counterspace, many of the activities and structures built into it serve to facilitate mutual understanding and support, and many of the relationships nurtured within the program offer BIPOC and female students a space to actively challenge oppressive forces.

Narrative Identity Work

The narratives people tell themselves about where they belong and what they are capable of (their storylines) become "a process through which individuals or collectives give meaning to themselves and others" (Case & Hunter, 2012, p. 262). Through narrative identity work, or work that actively resists traditional, oppressive narratives, it is possible to "bring about healing and restoration to marginalized individuals through contesting pejorative societal representations relative to these individuals and their reference groups" (Case & Hunter, 2012, p. 262). One way that PRISM has structurally incorporated narrative identity work involves support and promotion of students to aid in their ability to see themselves *as* scientists.

At the early stages of involvement, students receive funding to participate in undergraduate research, which not only helps to offset income lost to time in the laboratory but also validates students *as* academic researchers. While this does not fix all of the fiscal demands students have (Ruben still had to work 30 hours a week, for example, to pay for school and care for family), it certainly alleviates some of the burden. In addition to funding their research, PRISM also provides students with white laboratory coats (counteracting stereotypes of who is allowed to wear one) as well as promotional pins and embroidered graduation sashes. Though seemingly small acts, these items publicly mark students as part of the PRISM community and, by extension, the STEM community, acting as microinclusions and emphasizing that they belong. The research experience culminates in two instantiations that further validate and recognize students as scientists: the first, a publication known as the "Undergraduate Research Chronicle," and the second, a day-long undergraduate research symposium where students present their research to the public.

The "Undergraduate Research Chronicle" began in 2010 as a means to recognize the work students engage in as scholars. This full-color, glossy booklet dedicates half a letter-sized page to each individual student, where they provide a photograph of themselves (typically in the PRISM-embroidered laboratory coat), a short biography of what drew them to STEM, and then an abstract of their research. These texts are circulated widely and can be used by the students as evidence of their performance for graduate school and employment applications. Similarly, the annual symposium celebrates the accomplishments of all undergraduate researchers by providing a conference event that allows students to demonstrate their knowledge and scientific communication skills in an authentic setting. PRISM provides preparation for the symposium, including scientific poster workshops, public speaking rehearsals, and free printing of the students' finished, full-color scientific posters.

Entwined in all of these activities are scaffolded academic supports provided by the program: workshops on research skills, how to write the PRISM research proposal, effective scientific presentation for conferences, presenting research in scientific posters, and using scholarly databases to find scholarly articles. Guidance is provided for finding and applying to external summer research opportunities. For students nearing graduation and interested in applying to graduate school, assistance is offered in preparing for the MCAT and GRE as well as in composing personal statements and resumes for medical and graduate school. In some instances, students are assisted in finding financial supports to offset some of the costs involved.

In addition to these programmatic supports and one-on-one relationships between mentors and mentees, where reinforcing belonging and articulating disciplinary expectations objectively is key, students are also encouraged to participate in conferences such as the Annual Biomedical Research Conference for Minority Students (ABRCMS; now the Annual Biomedical Research Conference for Minoritized Scholars) and the Society for Advancement of Chicanos/Hispanics and Native Americans in Science (SACNAS). Conferences like ABRCMS and SACNAS are not only places where students can meet peers from across the nation and build personal networks but are also important professionalization opportunities that afford a space to secure internships and postgraduate opportunities with institutions and individuals who *actively value* a diverse STEM workforce. They bring representation to a new level. When people are minoritized within a specific space, having meaningful others who understand (and will not try to explain away) their lived experience is critical.

Actively, programmatically engaging with narrative identity work is a critical aspect of building inclusive STEM spaces because it serves as an external force to disrupt traditional ideological views of who belongs in STEM disciplines. It physically manifests alternatives to the "white male template" (Thomas, 2017) that permeates these spaces. By actualizing a space where historically marginalized students can see and hear themselves being represented and can learn about individuals like them who have contributed to their fields, educators create a space where students can turn toward potential futures and orient as members of the disciplinary community.

Discipline as a Cultural Artifact

Structurally, PRISM works to fill the gaps and offer support in areas typically assumed to be part of an achievement gap. Yet, in my work with the six student participants in this study, it became clear that academic supports and representation were not the complete solution to closing the opportunity gap in STEM education. The pedagogy and curriculum was also critical—particularly being taught to step back and see the discipline as a cultural artifact to be examined and challenged. Helping students enter a space without consciously and critically examining the ways in which the spaces have historically kept them out only sets underrepresented students up for failure.

The idea of curriculum and discourse as culture is not new. As Michael Vavrus (2008) has explained, "traditional curricular and instructional methods . . . have often been ineffective for students of color, immigrant children, and students from lower socioeconomic families" due to the curricular and institutional privileging of White, middle-class values and expectations (p. 49). As a result, pedagogical approaches such as culturally responsive pedagogy and antiracist pedagogy that take into account the cultural backgrounds and life experiences of students in the classroom through the acknowledgment and infusion of their backgrounds into the curriculum have evolved.

When students encounter a new discipline as novices, they are often intimidated by its culture. They are intimidated by the reading and writing practices, the discourse (which includes language and jargon), the methodologies used, the valuing of information, and (in some cases) the lack of representation they see of people who look and sound like them. For those in undergraduate research, there is the additional pressure of fear of failure and disappointing someone in a position of power (i.e., their mentor). At the start of her undergraduate research experience, for example, Chloe's anxieties about the work of the laboratory were particularly high. Though she had some experience with scientific writing in her courses, she recognized that the writing expected of her in her research experience would be quite different. "Hard," was how she described it when asked what she was expecting. "Writing in such a specific way. . . . You know, it just sounds like such a difficult process." As a first-generation college student from a lower socioeconomic background, Chloe was acutely aware of the language differences between her home discourse and the discourses of both college and science. "Everything in science," she explained, "has to be super, super specific and in a very specific order." "It's college," she would say whenever she was asked about the difficulty level of the reading and writing, acknowledging that the ways of communication in that space were far different from those used in her home social circles and also suggesting that true discursive skill in science was a long way out of her reach.

Ruben's orientation to scientific discourse was similar at the start of his research experience. He quickly learned that the "style that you have to use" was not what he had been taught in his coursework. Ruben was negotiating multiple discourse communities on a daily basis: at home, he and his family spoke Spanish exclusively; on the construction site, it was a combination of both English and Spanish in an informal working-class banter; in his courses, the discourse was more formal and academic; in the laboratory, the language was jargon-filled and specific to analytical chemistry. Attached to each of those discourses were specific ways of thinking and knowing and different rules of participation that quickly became evident.

The advantage that both Chloe and Ruben had in these early stages of undergraduate research was that they had mentors (Latinx women themselves) who recognized the culturally informed aspect of scientific discourse and, as such, were clear that this was new territory each student was entering. The students participating in this study experienced a wide variety of language-positioning during their undergraduate research experience. Some mentors adopted a view that students would pick up the discourse through immersion over time; others took to teaching it explicitly, to various degrees. What I found through this study is that explicitly teaching the reading and writing practices of the discipline (what I refer to as "mentored writing") had powerful effects on both students' rhetorical skill and their identities as scientists.

The practice of mentored writing—writing that is not simply shared with a more experienced writer but that is explicitly directed—is not a new concept by any means. It is quite common, for example, to see creative writers working with more seasoned writer and peer groups to workshop their writing in an effort to assess affect and experiment with rhetorical moves and form. This same practice undergirds much of writing center pedagogy, as well. However, in STEM disciplinary arenas, this is not as common a practice. The most successful mentors I observed had a strong awareness of their students' needs. Drs. Bianchi and Martinez, in particular, were exceptional at this and had developed an explicit, scaffolded approach to teaching the genres, rhetorical conventions, and critical reading necessary to successfully engage with others as a scientist—and they did so without hampering their research progress.

This scaffolding began with reading practices, providing students with selected articles meant to orient them to the research in which they will be involved. These articles included the mentors' own writing, which allowed the students to see how their mentors engaged with the community discursively. Importantly, the mentors discussed the readings with the students to ensure that they understood the context, learned how to identify important takeaways, and critically questioned the material. They also reinforced the recursive process of writing by talking about their own writing processes as well as telling students to revise data sheets from experiment to experiment and source new literature when new questions arose.

They read and commented on students' writing early and often, providing constructive feedback that drew attention to the disciplinary jargon, and they did so in such a way as to position the scientific discourse as another language, rather than some deficit in the student's knowledge base. Across all my research participants, when mentored writing was used as part of the research experience, students showed an improved understanding of genre purpose and conventions. Their ability to read and retain disciplinary knowledge from the primary literature increased. Importantly, the positioning of scientific discourse as a dialect of English to be learned, rather than something that should come naturally, allowed them to see communicating as a scientist as a code-switching activity rather than as the abandonment of their home discourse. This not only helped build rhetorical facility, but it also helped situate the students as insiders to the scientific community.

The ways in which mentors positioned the discourse and practices of their respective disciplines became an important factor in how students experienced and engaged with scientific discourse. When faculty mentors explicitly addressed the underrepresentation of BIPOC and women in science and created space for multiple identities to exist and intersect, they created a space where students who identified as members of racial or gender minority groups could see clearly that this underrepresentation is not correlated to some biological factor but has really been about access and erasure. When they did not recognize this historical positioning, students often interpreted their struggles as deficits within themselves.

Explicitly talking about these realities also helped to counteract the imposter syndrome that presented itself quite a bit for students in the early stages when they sensed that they were being given something just *because* they were a minority, not because they earned it. One exciting finding of this research that related to explicitly addressing disciplinary culture and history was that many students began to see their difference as power. They recognized that their social positioning provided them with a unique lens through which to view their work—viewpoints that represented large gaps in the field. In our final conversation, for example, Anne explained that her experience as a Black woman from a low-income family gave her agency within her home community and empowered her to pursue lines of research that were to date underexplored (maternal death rates for Black women). Something as simple as talking about the discipline's culture seemed to have powerful effects on students' self-concepts as STEM practitioners.

Direct Relational Transactions: Planning for Mentor Fit

The most profound impact UREs have in moving toward a counterspace relates to direct relational transactions, in which students have "a community of others who can empathize with their experiences, reducing alienation and exclusion" (Case & Hunter, 2012, p. 266). Building an understanding with peers and mentors of what it means to be a successful female and/or BIPOC scientist was critical in building self-efficacy for students in this study. Elsewhere in this book, I have placed strong emphasis on representation: the need for students to see people in positions of power who look and sound like them. Now, I would like to complicate that notion slightly. In the context of mentoring, fit is far more extensive than mentors and mentees sharing a similarity (for example, a shared area of study or interest, a shared gender or other demographic). As Vicki L. Baker and her coauthors (2014) note, "Fit is achieved through the presence of shared values, complementarity, and mutuality" (p. 84). Both the mentor and mentee must have a common goal and means to achieve that goal; each plays a role that benefits the relationship, and each offers something to the other. In short, fit is bidirectional, not unidirectional.

While fit has been of great concern to scholars working in organizational and management realms, it has largely focused on employer-employee relations and influence on productivity. But we know mentors play a *different* role than supervisors in the lives of students, and thus the mentor-mentee relationship requires "a different understanding of fit" Baker et al., 2014, p. 84). Those matching mentors with mentees need to take into account how the mentor views the relationship (including their expectations), how the student views the relationship, and where there is agreement and dissonance.

For example, it is not uncommon for students to enter the undergraduate research experience with an expectation that the experience will be akin to a directed study. They believe their mentors will spend time guiding them through the stages of research, telling them what to read, telling them when and what to write, etc. Those students enter with a specific set of assumptions and expectations. Similarly, it is not uncommon for mentors to have eight to ten other students working in their labs whom they expect to onboard the new students. As discussed previously, some mentors also believe that it is the students' duty to seek out scholarly literature related to the lab work and then propose a topic for research. These mentors' assumptions are that the students enter knowing that this needs to be done as well as how to do it.

In these instances, there is an enormous dissonance between the students and mentors. Depending on individuals' prior experiences as learners and teachers, they could begin to unintentionally make assumptions about one another. The mentors might find themselves saying, "This student is underprepared for research, so I need to give them simple tasks." Or, "This student isn't invested in the work." The students might think, "My mentor treats me like a child. I'm just a benchwarmer." Or, worse, "I don't think I belong here."

When mentors and mentees do not fit because of expectations and pedagogy, it can tear at the students' identities and reinforce the belief that they do not belong because, when students "fail" or fail to meet mentors' expectations, that failure often becomes internalized as evidence that they do not belong. Students do not necessarily recognize "failure" as simply not yet possessing the necessary skills to thrive within the undergraduate research context.

As mentors and faculty, we have a responsibility to make sure that our expectations and pedagogy are appropriate for the students working with us in undergraduate research and in our classroom settings. It is up to us to let students know outright what it will look like to work with us in research or to be in our classrooms, and it is up to us to decide whether we will alter our practices for a particular student when our default pedagogy may not seem to be working. Administrators of programs also have a role in helping students find mentors who are appropriate to their learning needs. It is not always about what subject of study the mentors examine or what gender or ethnicity they are, though if those can also be accommodated, all the better.

Providing Space for Resistance

Resistance—pushing back against—can look like problematic behavior when not viewed in full context. Ruben, as discussed in Chapter 4, resisted scientific discourse when he struggled to see a place for himself in the field. To his mentor, he looked disinterested and "checked out," but in many ways he was enacting resistance, making a concerted effort to not be changed by oppressive conditions (Case & Hunter, 2012, p. 259). In fields that are historically exclusionary, having a space to safely challenge discourse and behaviors that are experienced as oppressive is critical.

As noted earlier, one of the ways that STEM education is both critiqued and made accessible to students is through accepted uses of language. The Spanish-speaking students in this study felt as comfortable engaging with one another, mentors, and administrators in Spanish as they did in English. PRISM has taken steps to include Latinx communities by translating public-facing materials that may be read by families and friends outside of the college community (e.g., the invitation to the PRISM symposium). Equally common to hear in the laboratories and hallways are students speaking African American Vernacular English. Though seemingly a small act, speaking a language other than Academic English in STEM settings can be seen as an act of resistance to the English-dominated discourse.

Other areas where the culture of PRISM pushed against the norms were the inclusion of women and family. In academia broadly, and in STEM disciplines specifically, there is a strong push for women to put career before family (i.e., not get pregnant). Should women have children, they are expected to keep those children hidden so as not to be distracting (Barth et al., 2016; Economou, 2014; Plevkova et al., 2020). The faculty mentors (male and female) in PRISM, however, did not adhere to such rules. During this study, multiple female mentors became pregnant and embraced and celebrated their new family additions. Students in my study—particularly the female students—remarked that it was encouraging to see how a professional scientist could juggle the physical challenges of pregnancy with the rigor of laboratory work. When one laboratory had to cancel a trip to a conference due to the potential for exposure to Zika virus, students did not feel frustrated or inconvenienced. Instead, they worked to find an alternative opportunity and repurpose the abstracts and research for a conference closer to home. Further, it is not uncommon for students in laboratories to know their mentor's children and occasionally see them in the department. This familial, communal approach directly counteracted the narrative of scientists living and working alone with no time for a meaningful personal life.

Conclusion and Applications

The undergraduate research space is one where worlds, cultures, languages, and experiences come in contact with one another. Unlike Mary Louise Pratt's (1991) "contact zones," however, where cultures "meet, clash, and grapple with each other, often in contexts of highly asymmetrical relations of power" (p. 34), PRISM works actively to diffuse the tensions that may result from differences related to race/ethnicity, gender, socioeconomic status, and prior knowledge. While not perfect in its execution, using the URE space to allow power and disciplinary negotiations to take place creates an opportunity for students and faculty in PRISM to form affinity groups, build relationships, and create narratives that increase inclusion and accountability. During my study, the URE functioned as a safe space where minoritized individuals could counter dominant narratives of oppression prevalent in STEM disciplines and prevalent throughout their whole lives.

While it may not always be possible to address *all* of these mechanisms in a classroom, laboratory, or program, there are ways that educators and mentors can enact them on a smaller scale. Narrative identity work is about ensuring that students see themselves in the space they are attempting to enter. This includes representation in the educators and practitioners that they encounter, but it also means that their identities are represented in the texts and ideas encountered. As I noted in Chapter 2, Chloe's mention of learning briefly in one class about Rosalind Franklin's contribution to identifying the structure of DNA is insufficient. Educators should actively ask themselves about what gets privileged in their courses, whose perspectives are included, and what they can do to include more diverse voices.

Similarly, it is important that educators help students see the connections between community and language. Teaching students that the ways in which individuals communicate in analytical chemistry will differ from how they communicate in forensic entomology is a simple, yet powerful, way to help students orient to their fields. Providing explicit instruction on the rhetorical moves common to a field not only points out the differences between fields but also provides students with models for their own writing and helps them begin to recognize patterns when encountering new research texts. Languaging practices are not universal, and students from underrepresented backgrounds benefit from having tools to decode texts (while students from dominant backgrounds have their eyes opened to the many other ways of communicating that exist and are valid).

Finally, creating space for resistance—and *expecting* resistance—from newcomers can be generative. In disciplines that ask practitioners to support ideas through empirical research and to test ideas rigorously, faculty members and mentors have to provide space for that critical lens to be applied to the historical practices and beliefs of their fields, as well. This might entail actions as simple as challenging the accepted norms of what scientists physically look like or how they speak and write about their research. It might mean reconsidering research methods or considering alternative ways of knowing. It should involve helping students see that their life experiences and cultural backgrounds are not in conflict with their new disciplinary identity and could lead to generative queries and perspectives. In whatever manner it is actualized, it is important to provide opportunities for newcomers to be able to actively critique the conditions in which they are living, learning, and working and to call out and name oppressive forces when they are present (Jocson, 2006).

In the next, final chapter, I take up the practical applications that come from this research. Through continued discussion of how counterspaces work, I highlight five areas where program administrators and faculty can immediately focus attention to make their STEM educational spaces more inclusive and accountable. These recommendations not only are meant to reduce obstacles for students but also are meant to be achievable for faculty new to this work. They serve as entry points, not full solutions unto themselves.

Chapter 6. Building Equity
with Counterspaces

The process of guiding students into becoming members of disciplinary communities is not about stripping from them who and what they are and rebuilding but of merging their new selves into what is already there. As I have strived to illustrate in this book, it is not enough to create access and offer representation to BIPOC and female students in STEM education. Not creating spaces to critique the practices, ideologies, and obstacles of the disciplines risks efforts toward equity and inclusion being perceived as superficial, disingenuous, and/or tokenizing. While providing laboratory coats and bilingual promotional materials goes toward helping students feel seen as members of the STEM community, without also providing space to talk about their experience, without faculty mentors being mindful of inequity, and without the willingness to recognize the ways patriarchy and white supremacy are institutionalized, BIPOC and female STEM students will continue to "leak" from the "pipeline." One solution is to actively cultivate counterspaces.

PRISM as an institutionalized, undergraduate research program has done an excellent job of creating the structures and activities needed for a foundational counterspace (see Chapter 5), but the individual relationships with faculty mentors, peers, and administrators played an even more critical role in creating a counterspace because it was in these relationships that students were concretely positioned within their fields. This is not to say that all was perfect. As previous chapters showed, students experienced harm and problems persisted. But in those day-to-day, interpersonal exchanges, students learned how they belonged and/or had a future in STEM, and they developed self-concepts that allowed for adaptive responding.

In this final chapter, I suggest practical applications for beginning the work of undoing systemic bias and White Institutional Presence (WIP) within STEM laboratory spaces, with an intentional eye toward creating counterspaces, spaces where students can "consciously name the structural violence of our institutions" and disciplines (Kynard, 2018, p. 523) and collaborate on ways to counteract such forces. While it is impossible to distill down the process of achieving counterspaces into a checklist of steps to take and actions to perform, my aim is to provide recommendations to consider in light of an individual's own institution into which different elements might be incorporated. These recommendations have the potential to be modified for classroom spaces as well, and they serve as an entry-point toward making structural changes.

Conscious Acknowledgment of Student Orientation and Positioning

In Chapters 1 and 2, I discussed the ways in which individuals orient to the world, with a specific emphasis on disciplinary spaces. Importantly, I discussed the ways in which people's orientations to disciplinary spaces are influenced by multiple factors that impact how they position themselves within a space. As Walton and colleagues (2019) laid out in their work, these positions are influenced by factors such as

- who we are in relation to others (What does it mean to be a Black woman in a white-dominated field like science?),
- how our identities are working at the present time (How is being a Black female scientist different in 2021 than it was in 1980?),
- what it means to be occupying a particular role or space (What does being a good scientist look like for a Latinx woman? How does that change in differing environments?), and
- how our identities in these roles interact with normative expectations of who has historically occupied them (How does being Black or Latinx in science influence performance expectations? What assumptions are applied that are not applied to White individuals in the same space?).

Because these factors differ from individual to individual and can compound where oppressed identities intersect (Crenshaw, 1991), it is critical that faculty mentors and programs make explicit the ways in which these factors will likely influence students' experiences in STEM education. Pretending that they will not is simply a form of institutional gaslighting. Thus, a first step toward creating space for underrepresented individuals in a discipline is to learn about and openly and actively recognize the ways in which minoritized groups have historically been and are currently positioned within the discipline. (The works of Ebony Omotola McGee, 2020, and McGee and William H. Robinson, 2019, for example, offer excellent contemporary explorations into the lived experiences of racism and sexism in STEM; similarly, the works of Jeremiah J. Sims, 2018, and Kelly M. Mack and colleagues, 2019, offer strategies for culturally responsive approaches to STEM education.)

In this study, Natalia, for example, was deeply aware of the unique situation she was in by attending John Jay College: "It's pretty cool because usually, you would think, like, 'minorities in college,' that's really hard . . . difficult to find. But at John Jay, it's like, 'Not really!'" She allowed herself to just *be* in a space, as she put it, "where everyone is different." At the same time, however, Natalia was not naïve. On more than one occasion she wondered about some of the programs, including PRISM, which focused on increasing diversity in STEM, saying, "Just me being Hispanic, you know, just being a minority—I just have that intuition. Like, 'Oh, is it because I'm Hispanic [that I got this opportunity]?' So, you're thinking twice about it. And it's awful." She felt guilt at being able to apply for

summer programs that friends who were not "considered a minority" were ineligible for, wondering, "Am I getting something just because I'm a minority and
they want to show, like, 'Our percentages for minorities are getting higher!'" This
critical awareness, interestingly, translated into her dedication to *my* research. At
some point in every conversation, Natalia would comment about how excited she
was to be part of this project that would "help students like [her]" in the future
and help to improve science education for students of color and women. Though
she was excited to see how her own growth as a writer would play out, she seemed
more excited about the implications for the research. Importantly, the national
social climate during this period as well had palpable effects on her advocacy and
dedication to science. Natalia saw the results of the 2016 presidential election as
"pretty much supporting White *male* supremacy" as well as being anti-science,
and though she feared for her safety as a Latina and for her career opportunities
as a scientist, her positive attitude carried her through:

> I could drown in fear, but that does not help at all. . . . What I've
> been thinking about is just, like, I've worked so hard or this and
> someone has to recognize that. And I'm going to keep working
> hard for this so that—it should happen, at least. And not just
> for me, because I'm not the only person doing this. There are so
> many other people trying to get an opportunity to [do] research
> and [pursue] a career in science.

Being able to talk about these emotions and concerns with peers and her mentor helped Natalia step out of her own mind and experience and realize the larger
systems at play that contributed to her feeling the way she did. As Andrés Castro
Samayoa (2018) articulated about his research with undergraduates at diverse
institution types, "programs that center students' identities as a core component
of [their] programming can steward a more holistic understanding of how we
are to support those [who] will become the future of our academic profession"
(Conclusions section). Consciously acknowledging the positioning of minoritized individuals within a discipline creates space for them to then acknowledge
the obstacles that result.

Important in this acknowledgment and transparency are the experiences of
BIPOC and female faculty mentors in their *own* journey to become professionals.
While many faculty members may feel uncomfortable sharing the experiences
they had in the early stages of their academic careers, as these can make one
feel very vulnerable, such stories can serve as important orientation points for
minoritized students. The use of what Christina V. Cedillo and Phil Bratta (2019)
describe as "positionality stories"—the stories people tell "about their own lived
experiences" (p. 216)—by both faculty members *and* students can offer students
a way to orient themselves within the laboratory or classroom and can offer them
possible pathways and futures. Such stories can also help students see that some of
their experiences may not be unique to them. Discussions of how her writing was

torn apart by faculty advisors, for example, allowed Dr. Bianchi to show Amrita and Natalia that she did not enter her field an expert scientific writer. Her writing and research skills—which both students viewed as exceptional—were developed over time through trial, error, and revision and were not honed until after she had earned a PhD. Similarly, Dr. Martinez sharing with Ruben her understanding of his conflicting duties (as a student, father, and construction employee) allowed him to see that these different worlds did not necessarily have to be in competition with one another—that strategies exist for balancing and merging them in a healthy way.

Lifting the curtain on what becoming a member of the STEM community actually looks like for minoritized individuals complicates and diversifies the narratives of exceptionalism that students have been exposed to throughout their academic careers. Similarly, creating space for students to share stories of their experiences within a program provides the faculty and administrators an opportunity to understand what is working and areas for improvement.

Explicit Discussions of Rights, Duties, and Expectations

Part of people's understanding of how they are positioned within the hierarchies of a space relates to the rights and duties they see as belonging to them. What are they allowed to do? What is off limits? In this study, Anne, for example, did not feel that she had a right to infringe on her mentor's time or resources, and she saw her duty within the laboratory space (at the start) as that of a helper to others "who knew what they were doing." Natalia, on the other hand, believed that it was her duty as a student researcher to do independent work, and at a high caliber, before bringing it to Dr. Bianchi. The expectations for performance within the laboratory spaces, particularly with regard to what students should know to do and how, varied widely across student researchers and mentors. This applied to both the laboratory work of conducting research as well as the rhetorical aspects of writing.

Mentors being explicit with students about their specific roles within the research environment, the expectations of what they should be able to do upon entering, and the level of mentor involvement on the research work had positive impacts on students' sense of place in the undergraduate research experience. Knowing where they stood in relation to the faculty mentor and other members of the laboratory allowed students to then align those expectations with outside responsibilities. In examining the impact of reading and writing expectations on these student researchers, it became clear that personal, familial, and collegial expectations are all factors that can push students from, or pull them toward, their disciplines.

As I have written elsewhere (Falconer, 2019b; Falconer, in press), Ruben's was a complicated story. As a student juggling the demands of work, family, and school, he was in a constant state of flux that pulled his attention in a multitude of directions. Without a clear understanding of *why* he needed to do the reading and writing labor asked of him, he experienced a conflict with school-work-life balance that disrupted his skill development in scientific discourse. After recognizing how these various factors were affecting Ruben's success, his mentor adopted the approach of explicitly teaching the rhetorical moves and genres of science in a way that both helped Ruben see the discourse as something to be learned over time (and realize that it was within his grasp) and showed him how practicing the process of critical inquiry in undergraduate research would benefit him in all facets of his life.

Though no less labor-intensive, Chloe's experience involved a different type of personal conflict. Though she recognized the work she needed to do in order to succeed in the reading and writing practices of undergraduate research, and occasionally was self-deprecating about the amount of work that needed to be done, she was able to see with the help of her mentor a clear path forward. As Laura Wilder (2012) found in her study of faculty and students in introductory literature courses, making explicit the rhetorical conventions, genres, and purposes of disciplinary writing can help underprepared students access the rhetorical practices that lead to success within disciplinary contexts. Ruben and Chloe's stories help show how explicitly learning disciplinary rhetorical practices can also alleviate some of the anxiety and paralysis students might experience when encountering disciplinary texts early in their academic and professional careers.

Among the lessons learned from Ruben and Chloe's experiences is that coursework—advanced or introductory—does not always adequately prepare students for the realities of practicing their disciplines. Students are not typically taught in courses how to do discursive work or given tools to navigate new rhetorical contexts, and as a result, they encounter another threshold later in their academic careers—whether in undergraduate research or graduate work. For students who already experience the extra labor of being minoritized in their fields, this can feel defeating. If different disciplinary discourse practices are not made explicit, students can and will internalize their difficulties with them as personal deficits. Similarly, Chloe and Ruben's experiences showed that a heavy emphasis on grammar and mechanics can cause paralysis for students and slow down their willingness to engage with risk-taking when it comes to writing in new genres and discourses. The fear of getting things wrong can disrupt students' sense of competency, and revision requests without explicit direction and context can cause a home-school conflict whereby students perceive revision of their writing as unnecessary labor that interferes with their other commitments. Connected to these lessons is the fact that, as Chloe and Ruben showed, career identity and personal identity play critical roles in whether students will fully engage with new discourses and genres, particularly when there is significant labor involved. Program expectations that do not easily reconcile with the challenges that many BIPOC and female students encounter can disrupt the paths that they see as viable, and unless the reading and writing work requested has a useful application to their immediate or future selves, students questioning their place in the discipline may disengage with learning the discourse. As educators and mentors, there is ample reason to be conscious of these things in our teaching and undergraduate research experiences.

Challenge Existing Patterns of Belief and Assumed Norms

It can be deeply uncomfortable for faculty members and administrators to consciously critique disciplinary norms and assumptions about what the performativity of "scientist" looks like. In addition to the storylines that have been embedded socially over time (e.g., "boys are good at maths," "girls have better language skills"), it is important to actively question the ways in which disciplines are structured and how those structures are designed to keep certain people out.

In their research on compassion for distress, Rachel L. Ruttan and her colleagues (2015) examined the ways in which individuals who have endured emotional distress and *persisted* through that distress responded to others who endured a similar emotional distress but *failed to endure*, those "who [were] unable to overcome or appropriately cope" (p. 611). As they explained, the "hot–cold empathy gap" (or the inability to remember the impact of pain and discomfort while in a calm, unharmed state; Loewenstein, 1996) "suggests that difficulties recalling the impact of past emotional distress may lead people who have endured distress to be less compassionate toward others' failures to endure" (p. 611). In the context of undergraduate research experiences, this means it is critical for all participants to be willing to revisit discomfort and abandon narratives of grit. Far too often, programs use gatekeeping practices (i.e., threshold level grades for required courses) in order to "weed out" students who are not ready for or are not perceived as belonging in a major. These practices are often used to justify a lack of diversity in STEM spaces because it places the onus of performance on students and not the system. But, as I discussed in Chapter 2, WIP is deeply embedded in both educational and STEM disciplinary spaces, and a lack of acknowledgment about the real, immediate impacts these institutionalized biases have on newcomers to STEM fields means that little change can happen.

As faculty members and administrators working in educational programming meant to bring diversity, equity, and inclusion to disciplinary spaces, we have to remember that justice is a critical—and, likely, the most impactful—practice to take up. Without accountability to those we are attempting to aid, diversity, equity, and inclusion activities become merely performative. Accountability begins with acknowledging the history of the field. It continues with a close examination of the ways in which biases are institutionalized in our policies, practices, and programming. Accountability means that we need to be able to look actively at the ways in which we can reduce obstacles for newcomers, including challenging our own beliefs about our field, pushing against our desires to stick with what we know, being willing to provide the energy needed to make change happen, and confronting our own emotional responses to such change. It is deeply reflective and personal work.

Part of challenging our beliefs also relates directly to the students who are in our educational spaces. It is important to be mindful of meeting students where they are as well as mindful of our own assumptions and preconceived ideas about who these students are and what they are capable of. No two students are identical, and generalizing based on race/ethnicity, socioeconomic status, or gender is harmful. What seemed critical in this study with regard to how students transitioned through their experiences and developed discursive skill was the strong influence of how student participants positioned themselves (consciously or not) and how they were positioned by others. Preconceived ideas both of what *students* believed themselves capable of and what *others* believed them capable of influenced the power various push- and pull-factors had on their transitions from outsider to insider. Some students, such as Amrita, a woman and a person of color, will possess the power and agency to advocate for themselves in academic and professional contexts, while others, such as Anne, will not recognize that there is power or agency to wield. We must be careful not to view the success of one as evidence that *all* can succeed; positioning students within hierarchies of potential through the recognition of some identities (i.e., gender or ethnicity) may unintentionally mask other identities that influence academic performance (i.e., socioeconomic class and prior schooling influences).

Faculty Self-Reflection on Writing Development

As Bethany Davila (2017), Victor Villanueva (1993), and others have noted, the intentions of an instructor (in this case, faculty mentor) rarely matter when considering harm caused by race- and gender-evasive ideologies. Whether mentors argue for a presumed neutrality of Standard Academic English or recognize the bias inherent in it is irrelevant if their classroom and laboratory spaces reify and privilege oppressive discursive practices. While it is important, for instance, to recognize the linguistic bias that exists in scientific publishing and to prepare students for encountering this bias in their professional careers, it is also important that faculty members do not penalize students for not conforming to this bias along their journeys toward learning how to enact disciplinary discourse in a way that their fields will recognize.

This is not to suggest that it is more fair or even appropriate for faculty members to allow students to write disciplinary-specific texts for disciplinary spaces in whatever vernacular they wish but rather to suggest that faculty members should assist in their students' understanding of discourse community, code-switching, and code-meshing (Gumperz, 1982; Young et al., 2018). STEM spaces continue to be exclusionary, particularly in communicative realms like publishing, and if educators do not prepare students for the expectations of the fields they are entering, it sets those students up for failure. As part of their self-reflection, it is important for faculty members to remember their own literacy development as scholarly, scientific writers. In addition to reflecting on the literacy sponsors in their academic journeys, it is helpful for them to reflect on the different phases of discursive development they went through and to recognize that their students are currently going through the same, or similar, phases.

At the initial stage of entering a discourse community, students begin by experimenting, or "trying on" the discourse, attempting to write and speak in a way that approximates the writing and speaking practices of the community they are attempting to join. This engagement is influenced first and foremost by access to the discourse (e.g., through a course or internship that requires attempting to converse or write in the discourse). It is also influenced by culture and ideology (e.g., whether students see the discourse as a possibility for themselves and how far from their native discourse(s) this new one lies). In many ways, this process describes the stage of writing development highlighted in Lee Ann Carroll's *Rehearsing New Roles* (2002), in which students write and speak without the context or discourse knowledge required to compose rhetorically effective documents (p. 53). During this stage, there is a dissociation—a gap between how learners use language naturally and how the community they are attempting to enter uses language. This gap varies from individual to individual depending on how closely aligned their home discourse is to that of the new one (e.g., Standard American [Academic] English).

With experimentation, however, comes familiarization, and students begin to understand the rhetorical and discourse conventions of the community (e.g., what language and tone is acceptable, what genres are used in which contexts). This stage also involves beginning to learn the hierarchies of the rhetorical space in which they are circulating: Who is allowed to speak and in what manner? Roxanne Mountford (2001) explains that "rhetorical space is an extraordinarily important aspect of rhetorical performance," even more so in revered spaces (such as a laboratory), "where each object and participant are set in place according to the [practices] performed in that space" (p. 61–62). Within rhetorical spaces, individuals are expected to perform roles appropriate to their status in the hierarchy (e.g., a novice scientist does not make assertions about which methods are best). How quickly students learn these conventions is determined by the teaching methods of the mentor, the students' prior experiences with writing both within and outside of the community, their understandings of threshold concepts in writing, as well as their education levels and cultures. It is in this temporal space where explicit teaching can be particularly effective, because it is at this point that students begin to internalize the perceived discourse conventions and confront social associations *with* it. As Carroll (2002) notes, "knowing what to do [is] not the same as knowing how to do it" (p. 114). It is also not the same as knowing that you are *allowed* to do it. Such rights are deeply entwined with individuals' perceived status in the disciplinary community, their content knowledge, and their beliefs regarding language as a marker of identity generally.

If students understand an approximation of the rhetorical and discourse conventions of the community, with practice they develop facility with the discourse and continue to experiment and receive reinforcement or correction from experts/insiders. For undergraduates, this is a high bar to meet. For students with prior knowledge and exposure, like Natalia, it is possible to enter into a disciplinary experience with a sense of facility with disciplinary discourse. For others, however, expecting such an engagement from an undergraduate student at the start is unrealistic and unfair. As students' knowledge base solidifies, their development is then influenced by their affiliation with the community, their sense of belonging, as well as their commitment to and engagement with the discourse itself. Rather than attempting to "sound like" a member of the community, the student is *becoming* one and is beginning to adopt it as their own—taking responsibility for and ownership of it.

Adoption of the discourse is not assimilation. Rather, it is the taking up of an identity and the negotiation of that identity in relation to other identities. For example, a student might identify as a scientist *and* a woman of color *and* a first-generation college student. This identification includes external positioning and requires negotiating how much of the new identity to adopt, which discourse conventions will become part of the student's way of being, thinking, and communicating. At this stage, students have already encountered and begun to explore new ways of thinking and "alternative paths for a future. . . . They are," as Anne J. Herrington and Marcia Curtis (2000) described, "looking for sponsoring frameworks" (p. 125). Students are seeking structured approaches "through which they can pursue their interests . . . .[and] are reflecting on their families and pasts, sorting through and trying to shape how that past fits with their present and future" (Herrington and Curtis, 2000, p. 125).

When that negotiation and reconciliation has been accomplished and ownership claimed, individuals are in a place to critique and manipulate the discourse to suit their own practical and ideological needs. Here, we can see instances of "writing against the grain" of the community, but in such a way as to still be acceptable. All discourse communities, to paraphrase John Swales (1990), have mechanisms of communication and participation, with specific lexes and genres, which are in service to maintaining the community's broadly agreed-upon set of goals (pp. 24–27). These communities rely on a certain "threshold level of members with a suitable degree of relevant content and discoursal expertise," (p. 27) thus there is a significant amount of individual agency at this stage, as individuals are *part* of the community that sets the norms. It is critical for faculty members to remember that *they* are members of that community, but their students are not. Through their own writing and review work, research faculty members have the power to question and critique the language and research practices of their respective fields. They can choose to push back against linguistic bias and other forms of discrimination to help disrupt institutionalized practices that create barriers. As the culture of those in power diversifies, so do the expectations. But their students are not in a position to hold such power and must be guided in meeting the demands of their fields in their current states.

Recognition and Planning Around Systemic Inequity

The final recommendation I offer is for faculty and administrators to engage in strategic planning to consciously address inequity. Building counterspaces requires significant critical reflection on the part of faculty and program administrators. It also requires an understanding of the practices and changes that are possible within the constructs of academic and disciplinary settings. Certainly it is not feasible to attempt all things at once because lasting change takes time, money, and energy to counter the very real forces that cause inertia and reinforce the status quo. Strategically, then, it becomes important to put time and energy into the changes most likely to be achievable while also attempting to address multiple points of friction students are likely to encounter along their academic journeys. In addition to the considerations mentioned above, program designers can consider the following in their programmatic efforts:

Representation

As much as possible, students should encounter individuals in positions of authority who look and sound like them. In undergraduate research settings, this means having faculty mentors who come from a wide variety of backgrounds and who represent different gender and linguistic identities. However, representation should also be evident in the curriculum. Recommendations to diversify and decolonize syllabi are widely available (e.g., Fuentes et al., 2021; Ruiz & Baca, 2017), but what is important to note, here, is that this work should be authentic and not performative. Faculty members should ensure that, without tokenizing or minimizing, they are drawing attention to BIPOC and female scientists who have made important contributions to the state of knowledge. Their inclusion should fit seamlessly within the curriculum. Epistemological and methodological diversity can be woven into discussions of the ways in which research is conducted (considering Indigenous, Arabic, and other cultural influences as appropriate). Discussions can also be held about who is helped and who is harmed by the choices researchers make.

Linguistic Awareness

Since publication is the currency of STEM disciplines, active discussions around the publication process is important if students are being prepared for careers in research. These discussions must include explicit instruction on how to write scientific genres, including actively teaching the linguistic features and genres students are most likely to read and write as part of their communicative work. In addition to mentored writing, however, linguistic bias should also be discussed so as to prepare students for potential challenges they may encounter. Importantly, faculty should choose writing assessment practices that are fair, equitable, and appropriate for students at different levels of their academic career (see Inoue, 2019; Poe et al,, 2018).

Recognize Competing Demands

Faculty members are well-versed in the challenges of managing competing demands for time, energy, and resources. It is critical to remember that students also have competing demands that impact their performance in classrooms and laboratories. Some of these demands may be related to caring duties, such as for family members or children. Some of these may be economic, such as the need to work in order to pay for school or contribute to the home. As much as possible, programs should account for the ways in which students may be pulled in multiple directions. Whenever possible, offering funding (as PRISM does) to offset the time students spend in the laboratory can help address economic impacts. Similarly, the use of open educational resources and providing access to scholarly research when it would otherwise be behind a paywall are inclusive approaches that can reduce economic demands. Providing frameworks for managing work-family-education balance can also be beneficial. Modeling what an appropriate amount of time in a laboratory is, for example, and setting clear boundaries for time at home can help students see that it is okay to not respond to texts or emails about research during dedicated family time.

Mentor-Student Pairing

In UREs, programs should think carefully and consciously about how students are paired with mentors. As discussed in Chapter 5, these pairings have important implications for students entering a disciplinary community as researchers. Short surveys around student interests, for example, are excellent, but these should be accompanied by questions about times when students learned well and times when they did not in order to understand the pedagogical approaches that are most likely to benefit them. Pairing students with mentors based solely on identity markers or areas of research interest has the potential to be problematic if other elements are not taken into consideration. Additionally, it should not be left to students to seek out and acquire their own mentors, as that creates a space for rejection, misalignment, and potential harm.

Conscious Construction of Counterspaces

While all of the elements discussed in this chapter can contribute to the construction of counterspaces, it is important to create physical spaces that allow individuals from communities marginalized in STEM disciplines to form affinity groups and "reflect on the uniqueness of their identity" within those disciplines (Flores, 1996, p. 146). As Lisa A. Flores (1996) noted, such spaces allow for the "rejection of dominant definitions and the affirmation of self identity" (p. 146), which can aid with coping and resistance to microaggressions and oppressions experienced within the respective educational spaces. To reduce microaggressions, programs should think actively about how to normalize the diverse identities and ways of creating knowledge that exist within STEM disciplines, highlighting the mechanisms through which various identities influence how people view the world and what they value.

Conclusion

As Ibram X. Kendi (2019) has explained, being antiracist is not about simply *not* being racist. It is about actively working in the moment to redress racism as it arises. In this book, I have worked to let the student participants' experiences and voices provide the insight needed to unpack what systematized racism and sexism looks like in practice. The invisibility of these forces means that they are powerful. However, actively engaging with them, critiquing our assumptions of what is "normal," and challenging practices that are exclusionary is one way of taking steps toward an antiracist (and antisexist, anticlassist, etc.) approach to disciplinary instruction.

This work is not about casting blame on any particular group of people. Rather, it is about lifting the curtain on the ways inequality is masked, often with good intentions. In my work with STEM faculty over the years, only once did I encounter an individual who espoused explicitly racist or sexist beliefs. All others were open about wanting to make their educational spaces more equitable while maintaining the rigor of their disciplines. Unfortunately, the good intentions of these faculty members sometimes led to practices that caused more harm than good.

Like other accommodation work, the aim for inclusion and accountability in STEM education is not to create more work for instructors. It is about reducing the obstacles, the points of friction, underrepresented students experience along their academic journeys in STEM education that overrepresented (White male) students do *not* experience. Like good design, addressing the issues that affect some will more often than not benefit all. As noted multiple times throughout, this work is only a continuation of the work of others who have come before me— and there is still so much to be learned. Deeper investigations are long overdue, for instance, into the resistance that exists in STEM disciplines toward making effective changes. Understanding how efforts like PRISM's transfer outside of UREs, such as to graduate programs and industry, is also in need. What happens to students once they leave these programs? How do STEM disciplines and workplaces, broadly, respond to their identities and perspectives?

Since this research was conducted, PRISM has gone on to make further modifications to its program that align with John Jay College's overall commitment to antiracist teaching and justice. Of the students who participated in this study,

Anne, Madalyn, Amrita, and Natalia have all gone on to graduate programs in STEM. Ruben sought laboratory work but instead took on a foreman's role in construction that provided a stable income for his family. He is still considering a master's degree in the future. Chloe, also, took a break from school and spent time working to help her family. As of this writing, she has not yet attempted to pursue a PhD.

References

Ahmed, S. (2006). *Queer phenomenology: Orientations, objects, others*. Duke University Press. https://doi.org/10.1215/9780822388074.

angetworld. (2014, April 21). *Neil Degrasse Tyson on being black, and women in science*. YouTube. Retrieved September 26, 2022, from https://www.youtube.com/watch?v=z7ihNLEDiuM.

Arana, R., Castañeda-Sound, C., Blanchard, S. & Aguilar, T. E. (2011). Indicators of persistence for Hispanic undergraduate achievement: Toward an ecological model. *Journal of Hispanic Higher Education, 10*(3), 237–251. https://doi.org/10.1177/1538192711405058.

Armstrong, J. (2020, March 11). Don't believe the myth that black people can't get coronavirus. *The Philadelphia Inquirer*. https://www.inquirer.com/health/coronavirus/coronavirus-blacks-african-americans-myths-philly-jenice-armstrong-20200310.html.

Austin, J. L. (1975). *How to do things with words* (2nd ed.). Harvard University Press.

Baber, L. D. (2019). Color-blind liberalism in postsecondary STEM education. In E. O. McGee & W. H. Robinson (Eds.), *Diversifying STEM: Multidisciplinary perspectives on race and gender* (pp. 19–36). Rutgers University Press.

Baker, V. L., Pifer, M. J. & Griffin, K. A. (2014). Mentor-protégé fit: Identifying and developing effective mentorship across identities in doctoral education. *International Journal for Researcher Development, 5*(2), 83–98. https://doi.org/10.1108/IJRD-04-2014-0003.

Baker-Bell, A. (2020). *Linguistic justice: Black language, literacy, identity, and pedagogy*. Routledge. https://doi.org/10.4324/9781315147383.

Bandura, A. (1997). *Self-efficacy: The exercise of control*. W. H. Freeman and Company.

Barth, J. M., Dunlap, S. & Chappetta, K. (2016). The influence of romantic partners on women in STEM majors. *Sex Roles, 75*, 110–125. https://doi.org/10.1007/s11199-016-0596-z.

Barton, A. C. (2001). Science education in urban settings: Seeking new ways of praxis through critical ethnography. *Journal of Research in Science Teaching, 38*(8), 899–917. https://doi.org/10.1002/tea.1038.

Beaufort, A. (2007). *College writing and beyond: A new framework for university writing instruction*. Utah State University Press.

Bell, D. (1992). *Faces at the bottom of the well: The permanence of racism*. Basic Books.

Bhabha, H. K. (1994). *The location of culture*. Routledge.

Bird, S. R. (2011). Unsettling universities' incongruous, gendered bureaucratic structures: A case-study approach. *Gender, Work and Organization, 18*(2), 202–30. https://doi.org/10.1111/j.1468-0432.2009.00510.x.

Bonilla-Silva, E. (2002). The linguistics of color blind racism: How to talk nasty about Blacks without sounding "racist." *Critical Sociology, 28*(1–2), 41–64. https://doi.org/10.1177/08969205020280010501.

Bonilla-Silva, E. (2018). *Racism without racists: Color-blind racism and racial inequality in contemporary America* (5th ed.). Rowman and Littlefield.

Boyatzis, R. E. (1998). *Transforming qualitative information: Thematic analysis and code development.* SAGE Publications.

Brandt, A. M. (1978). Racism and research: The case of the Tuskegee Syphilis study. *The Hastings Center Report, 8*(6), 21–29. http://nrs.harvard.edu/urn-3:HUL.Inst Repos:3372911.

Brandt, D. (1998). Sponsors of literacy. *College Composition and Communication, 49*(2), 165–185. https://library.ncte.org/journals/CCC/issues/v49-2/3181.

Brandt, D. (2015). *The rise of writing: Redefining mass literacy.* Cambridge University Press. https://doi.org/10.1017/CBO9781316106372.

Britton, D. M. (2010). Engendering the university through policy and practice: Barriers to promotion to full professor for women in the science, engineering, and math disciplines. In B. Riegraf, B. Aulenbacher, E. Kirsch-Auwärter & U. Müller (Eds.), *Gender change in academia: Re-mapping the fields of work, knowledge, and politics from a gender perspective* (pp. 15–26). VS Verlag für Sozialwissenschaften. https://doi.org/10.1007/978-3-531-92501-1_2.

Brown, B. A., Reveles, J. M. & Kelly, G. J. (2005). Scientific literacy and discursive identity: A theoretical framework for understanding science learning. *Science Education, 89*(5), 779–802. https://doi.org/10.1002/sce.20069.

Burchard, E. G., Oh, S. S., Foreman, M. G. & Celedón, J. C. (2015). Moving toward *true* inclusion of racial/ethnic minorities in federally funded studies. A key step for achieving respiratory health equality in the United States. *American Journal of Respiratory and Critical Care Medicine, 191*(5), 514–521. https://doi.org/10.1164/rccm.201410-1944PP.

Burgess, A. & Ivanič, R. (2010). Writing and being written: Issues of identity across timescales. *Written Communication, 27*(2), 228–255. https://doi.org/10.1177/0741088310363447.

Butler, J. (1997). *Excitable speech: A politics of the performative.* Routledge.

Carlone, H. B. & Johnson, A. (2007). Understanding the science experiences of successful women of color: Science identity as an analytic lens. *Journal of Research in Science Teaching, 44*(8), 1187–1218. https://doi.org/10.1002/tea.20237.

Carpi, A., Ronan, D. M., Falconer, H. M & Lents, N. H. (2013a). *I would have never thought this was possible for me: Creating a community of scientists at a Minority-serving institution through mentored undergraduate research.* Unpublished article.

Carpi, A., Ronan, D. M., Falconer, H. M., Boyd, H. H. & Lents, N. H. (2013b). Development and implementation of targeted STEM retention strategies at a Hispanic-serving institution. *Journal of Hispanic Higher Education, 12*(3), 280–299. https://doi.org/10.1177/1538192713486279.

Carpi, A., Ronan, D. M., Falconer, H. M. & Lents, N. H. (2017). Cultivating minority scientists: Undergraduate research increases self-efficacy and career ambitions for underrepresented students in STEM. *Journal of Research in Science Teaching, 54*(2), 169–194. https://doi.org/10.1002/tea.21341.

Carroll, L. A. (2002). *Rehearsing new roles: How college students develop as writers.* Southern Illinois University Press. https://wac.colostate.edu/books/ncte/carroll/.

Casanave, C. P. (2002). *Writing games: Multicultural case studies of academic literacy practices in higher education.* Lawrence Erlbaum Associates.

Case, A. D. & Hunter, C. D. (2012). Counterspaces: A unit of analysis for understanding the role of settings in marginalized individuals' adaptive responses to oppression. *American Journal of Community Psychology, 50*(1–2), 257–270. https://doi.org/10.1007/s10464-012-9497-7.

Cedillo, C. V. & Bratta, P. (2019). Relating our experiences: The practice of positionality stories in student-centered pedagogy. *College Composition and Communication, 71*(2), 215–240. https://library.ncte.org/journals/CCC/issues/v71-2/30421.

Chambers, D. W. (1983). Stereotypic images of the scientist: The draw-a-scientist test. *Science Education, 67*(2), 255–265. https://doi.org/10.1002/sce.3730670213.

Clavero, M. (2011). Unfortunately, linguistic injustice matters. *Trends in Ecology and Evolution, 26*(4), 156–157. https://doi.org/10.1016/j.tree.2011.01.011.

Cobb, J. P. (1976). Foreword. In S. M. Malcom, P. Q. Hall & J.W. Brown (Eds.), *The double bind: The price of being a minority woman in science: Report of a conference of minority women scientists* (AAAS Report No. 76-R-3) (pp. ix–x). ERIC. http://files.eric.ed.gov/fulltext/ED130851.pdf.

Coil, D., Wenderoth, M. P., Cunningham, M. & Dirks, C. (2010). Teaching the process of science: Faculty perceptions and an effective methodology. *CBE Life Sciences Education, 9*(4), 524–535. https://doi.org/10.1187/cbe.10-01-0005.

Collins, P. H. (2000). *Black feminist thought: Knowledge, consciousness, and the politics of empowerment* (2nd ed.). Routledge. https://doi.org/10.4324/9780203900055.

Cooper, J. E., He, Y. & Levin, B. B. (2011). *Developing critical cultural competence: A guide for 21st-century educators.* Corwin.

Cooperative Institutional Research Program. (2010). *Degrees of success: Bachelor's degree completion rates among initial STEM majors.* University of California, Higher Education Research Institute. https://heri.ucla.edu/nih/downloads/2010-Degrees-of-Success.pdf.

Crenshaw, K. (1989). Demarginalizing the intersection of race and sex: A Black feminist critique of antidiscrimination doctrine, feminist theory and antiracist politics. *The University of Chicago Legal Forum, 1989*, Article 8. http://chicagounbound.uchicago.edu/uclf/vol1989/iss1/8.

Crenshaw, K. (1991). Mapping the margins: Intersectionality, identity politics, and violence against women of color. *Stanford Law Review, 43*(6), 1241–1299. https://doi.org/10.2307/1229039.

Cresswell, J. W. (2013). *Qualitative inquiry and research design: Choosing among five approaches* (3rd ed.). SAGE Publications.

Cudd, A. E. (2001). Objectivity and ethno-feminist critiques of science. In K. M. Ashman & P. S. Baringer (Eds.), *After the science wars: Science and the study of science* (pp. 79–96). Routledge.

Davies, B. & Harré, R. (1990). Positioning: The discursive production of selves. *Journal for the Theory of Social Behavior, 20*(1), 43–63. https://doi.org/10.1111/j.1468-5914.1990.tb00174.x.

Davila, B. (2017). Standard English and colorblindness in composition studies: Rhetorical constructions of racial and linguistic neutrality. *WPA: Writing Program Administration, 40*(2), 154–173. http://associationdatabase.co/archives/40n2/40n2davila.pdf.

Davis, P. C. (1989). Law as microaggression. *Yale Law Journal, 98*(8), 1559–1577. http://hdl.handle.net/20.500.13051/16630.

Deci, E. L. & Ryan, R. M. (1985). *Intrinsic motivation and self-determination in human behavior.* Plenum Press.

DeCuir-Gunby, J. T., Chapman, T. K. & Schutz, P. A. (2019). Critical race theory, racial justice, and education. In J. T. DeCuir-Gunby, T. K. Chapman & P. A. Schutz (Eds.), *Understanding critical race research methods and methodologies: Lessons from the field* (pp. 3–10). Routledge.

Dee, T. & Penner, E. (2017). The causal effects of cultural relevance: Evidence from an ethnic studies curriculum. *American Educational Research Journal, 54*(1), 127–166. https://doi.org/10.3102/0002831216677002.

Delpit, L. (2006). *Other people's children: Cultural conflict in the classroom* (rev. ed.). The New Press.

Delpit, L. & Dowdy, J. K. (Eds.). (2002). *The skin that we speak: Thoughts on language and culture in the classroom.* The New Press.

DiAngelo, R. (2018). *White fragility: Why it's so hard for white people to talk about racism.* Beacon Press.

Diekmann, S. & Peterson, M. (2013). The role of non-epistemic values in engineering models. *Science and Engineering Ethics, 19*(1), 207–218. https://doi.org/10.1007/s11948-011-9300-4.

Economou, James S., MD, PhD. (2014). Gender bias in biomedical research. *Surgery, 156*(5), 1061–1065. https://doi.org/10.1016/j.surg.2014.07.005.

Fairclough, N. (1992). Discourse and text: Linguistic and intertextual analysis within discourse analysis. *Discourse and Society, 3*(2), 193–217. https://doi.org/10.1177/0957926592003002004.

Falconer, H. M. (2019a). "I think when I speak, I don't sound like that": The influence of social positioning on rhetorical skill development in science. *Written Communication, 36*(1), 9–37. https://doi.org/10.1177/0741088318804819.

Falconer, H. M. (2019b). Mentored writing at a Hispanic-serving institution: Improving student facility with scientific discourse. In I. Baca, Y. I. Hinojosa & S. W. Murphy (Eds.), *Bordered writers: Latinx identities and literacy practices at Hispanic-serving institutions* (pp. 213–230). State University of New York Press.

Falconer, H. M. (in press). Playing the expectation game: Negotiating disciplinary discourse in undergraduate research. In K. Ritter (Ed.), *Beyond fitting in: Rethinking first-generation writing and literacy education.* Modern Language Association.

Faulkner, W. (2007). 'Nuts and bolts and people': Gender-troubled engineering identities. *Social Studies of Science, 37*(3), 331–356. https://doi.org/10.1177/0306312706072175.

Faulkner, W. (2008). The gender(s) of 'real' engineers: Journey around the technical/social dualism. In P. Lucht & T. Pualitz (Eds.), *Recodierungen des wissens: Stand und perspektiven der geschlechterforschung in naturwissenschaften un technik*

[Recodings of knowledge: State and perspectives of gender studies in the natural sciences and technology]. Campus.

Faulkner, W. (2011). Gender (in)authenticity, belonging and identity work in engineering. *Brussels Economic Review/Cahiers Economiques de Bruxelles, 54*(2/3), p. 277–293. https://dipot.ulb.ac.be/dspace/bitstream/2013/108954/1/ARTICLE%20 FAULKNER.pdf.

Flores, L. A. (1996). Creating discursive space through a rhetoric of difference: Chicana feminists craft a homeland. *Quarterly Journal of Speech, 82*(2), 142–156. https://doi.org/10.1080/00335639609384147.

Fuentes, M. A., Zelaya, D. G. & Madsen, J. W. (2021). Rethinking the course syllabus: Considerations for promoting equity, diversity, and inclusion. *Teaching of Psychology, 48*(1), 69–79. https://doi.org/10.1177/0098628320959979.

García de Müeller, G. & Ruiz, I. (2017). Race, silence, and writing program administration: A qualitative study of US college writing programs. *WPA: Writing Program Administration, 40*(2), 19–39. http://associationdatabase.co/archives /40n2/40n2mueller_ruiz.pdf.

Gawthrop, E. (2022, August 16). *The color of coronavirus: COVID-19 deaths by race and ethnicity in the U.S.* APM Research Lab. https://www.apmresearchlab.org /covid/deaths-by-race.

Gay, G. (2010). *Culturally responsive teaching: Theory, research, and practice* (2nd ed.). Teachers College Press.

Gee, J. P. (2000). Identity as an analytic lens for research in education. *Review of Research in Education, 25*(1), 99–125. https://doi.org/10.3102%2F0091732X02 5001099.

Gee, J. P. (2001). Reading as situated language: A sociocognitive perspective. *Journal of Adolescent & Adult Literacy, 44*(8), 714–725. http://www.jstor.org/stable/40018744.

Gilbert, A.-F. (2009). Disciplinary cultures in mechanical engineering and materials science: Gendered/gendering practices? *Equal Opportunities International, 28*(1), 24–35. https://doi.org/10.1108/02610150910933613.

Gillborn, D. (2006). Critical race theory and education: Racism and anti-racism in educational theory and praxis. *Discourse: Studies in the Cultural Politics of Education, 27*(1), 11–32. https://doi.org/10.1080/01596300500510229.

Gilyard, K. (1991). *Voices of the self: A study of language competence.* Wayne State University Press.

Giroux, H. A. (1988). *Schooling and the struggle for public life: Critical pedagogy in the modern age.* University of Minnesota Press.

Guess, T. J. (2006). The social construction of whiteness: Racism by intent, racism by consequence. *Critical Sociology, 32*(4), 649–673. https://doi.org/10.1163/1569163 06779155199.

Gumperz, J. J. (1982). *Discourse strategies.* Cambridge University Press. https://doi .org/10.1017/CBO9780511611834.

Gusa, D. L. (2010). White institutional presence: The impact of whiteness on campus climate. *Harvard Educational Review, 80*(4), 464–489. https://doi.org/10.17763 /haer.80.4.p5j483825u110002.

Gutiérrez, K. D., Baquedano-López, P., Alvarez, H. H. & Chiu, M. M. (1999).

Building a culture of collaboration through hybrid language practices. *Theory into Practice, 38*(2), 87–93. https://doi.org/10.1080/00405849909543837.

Haas, M., Koeszegi, S. T. & Zedlacher, E. (2016). Breaking patterns? How female scientists negotiate their token role in their life stories. *Gender, Work and Organization, 23*(4), 397–413. https://doi.org/10.1111/gwao.12124.

Handelsman, J., and Smith, M. (2016, February 11). *STEM for All.* The White House: President Barack Obama. https://obamawhitehouse.archives.gov/blog/2016/02/11/stem-all.

Hansen, M., Schoonover, A., Skarica, B., Harrod, T., Bahr, N. & Guise J.-M. (2019). Implicit gender bias among US resident physicians. *BMC Medical Education, 19*, Article 396. https://doi.org/10.1186/s12909-019-1818-1.

Harré, R. (2004). Positioning theory. *Self-Care, Dependent-Care and Nursing, 16*(1), 28–32. https://oreminternationalsociety.org/s/Vol16No1January2008.pdf.

Harré, R. (2009). *Pavlov's dogs and Schrödinger's cat: Scenes from the living laboratory.* Oxford University Press.

Harré, R. & Moghaddam, F. (2003). Introduction: The self and others in traditional psychology and in positioning theory. In R. Harre and F. Moghaddam (Eds.), *The self and others: Positioning individuals and groups in personal, political, and cultural contexts* (pp. 1–12). Praeger Publishers.

Herrington, A. J. & Curtis, M. (2000). *Persons in process: Four stories of writing and personal development in college* (ED437670). ERIC. http://files.eric.ed.gov/fulltext/ED437670.pdf.

Holdcroft, A. (2007). Gender bias in research: How does it affect evidence based medicine? *Journal of the Royal Society of Medicine, 100*(1), 2–3. https://doi.org/10.1177/014107680710000102.

Holloway, W. (1984). Gender difference and the production of subjectivity. In J. Henriques, W. Holloway, C. Urwin, C. Venn & V. Walkerdine (Eds.), *Changing the subject: Psychology, social regulation and subjectivity* (pp. 11–25). Methuen and Company.

hooks, b. (1990). *Yearning: Race, gender, and cultural politics.* South End Press.

Hyland, K. (2012). *Disciplinary identities: Individuality and community in academic discourse.* Cambridge University Press.

Hyland, K. (2005). Stance and engagement: A model of interaction in academic discourse. *Discourse Studies, 7*(2), 173–192. https://doi.org/10.1177/1461445605050365.

Inoue, A. B. (2019). 2019 CCCC Chair's address: How do we language so people stop killing each other, or what do we do about White language supremacy? *College Composition and Communication, 71*(2), 352–369. https://library.ncte.org/journals/CCC/issues/v71-2/30427.

Inoue, A. B & Poe, M. (Eds.). (2012). *Race and writing assessment.* Peter Lang.

Inoue, A.B & Poe, M. (2020). How to stop harming students: An ecological guide to antiracist writing assessment. *Composition Studies, 48*(3), 1–5. https://compositionstudiesjournal.files.wordpress.com/2021/01/poeinoue_full.pdf.

Institutional Service. (2021, June 2). *Minority Science and Engineering Improvement Program.* U.S. Department of Education, Office of Postsecondary Education. https://www2.ed.gov/programs/iduesmsi/index.html.

Institutional Service. (2022, September 6). *Developing Hispanic-Serving Institutions Program—Title V*. U.S. Department of Education, Office of Postsecondary Education. https://www2.ed.gov/programs/idueshsi/index.html.

Ivanič, R. (1998). *Writing and identity: The discoursal construction of identity in academic writing*. John Benjamins.

Jocson, K. M. (2006). "The best of both worlds": Youth poetry as social critique and form of empowerment. In S. Ginwright, P. Noguera & J. Cammarota (Eds.), *Resistance! Youth activism and community change: New democratic possibilities for practice and policy for America's youth* (pp. 129–148). Routledge.

John Jay College on the Move. (2006). *The Hispanic Outlook in Higher Education Magazine, 17*, 35–37.

Jones, C. E. & Barco Medina, G. (2021). Teaching racial literacy through language, health, and the body: Introducing bio-racial rhetorics in the writing classroom. *College English, 84*(1), 58–77. https://library.ncte.org/journals/CE/issues/v84-1/31452.

Kachchaf, R., Ko, L., Hodari, A. & Ong, M. (2015). Career-life balance for women of color: Experiences in science and engineering academia. *Journal of Diversity in Higher Education, 8*(3), 175–191. https://doi.org/10.1037/a0039068.

Kahle, J. B. (1988). Gender and science education II. In P. Fensham (Ed.), *Development and dilemmas in science education* (pp. 249–265). Routledge.

Keels, M. (2019). *Campus counterspaces: Black and Latinx students' search for community at historically white universities*. Cornell University Press. https://doi.org/10.7591/cornell/9781501746888.001.0001.

Kelly, A. (1985). The construction of masculine science. *British Journal of Sociology of Education, 6*(2), 133–153. https://doi.org/10.1080/0142569850060201.

Kendi, I. X. (2019). *How to be an antiracist*. One World.

Keville, T. D. (1994). The invisible woman: Gender bias in medical research. *Women's Rights Law Reporter, 15*, 123–142.

Konkel L. (2015). Racial and ethnic disparities in research studies: The challenge of creating more diverse cohorts. *Environmental Health Perspectives, 123*(12), A297–A302. https://doi.org/10.1289/ehp.123-A297.

Kreps, S. E. & Kriner, D. (2020). *Medical misinformation in the COVID-19 pandemic*. SSRN. https://doi.org/10.2139/ssrn.3624510.

Kynard, C. (2018). Stayin woke: Race-radical literacies in the makings of a higher education. *College Composition and Communication, 69*(3), 519–529. https://library.ncte.org/journals/CCC/issues/v69-3/29491.

Ladson-Billings, G. & Tate, W. F., IV. (1995). Toward a critical race theory of education. *Teachers College Record, 97*(1), 47–68. https://doi.org/10.1177/016146819509700104.

Lave, J. & Wenger, E. (1991). *Situated learning: Legitimate peripheral participation*. Cambridge University Press. https://doi.org/10.1017/CBO9780511815355.

Lederman, N. G. (1992). Students' and teachers' conceptions of the nature of science: A review of the research. *Journal of Research in Science Teaching, 29*(4), 331–359. https://doi.org/10.1002/tea.3660290404.

Lee, E. Y., Lin, J., Noth, E. M., Hammond, S. K., Nadeau, K. C., Eisen, E. A. & Balmes, J. R. (2017). Traffic-Related Air Pollution and Telomere Length in

Children and Adolescents Living in Fresno, CA: A Pilot Study. *Journal of Occupational and Environmental Medicine, 59*(5), 446–452. https://doi.org/10.1097/JOM .0000000000000996.

Lefebvre, H. (1991). *The production of space* (D. Nicholson-Smith, Trans.). Basil Blackwell. (Original work published 1974)

Lemke, J. L. (1990). *Talking science: Language, learning, and values.* Ablex.

Lerchenmueller, M. J. & Sorenson, O. (2018). The gender gap in early career transitions in the life sciences. *Research Policy, 47*(6), 1007–1017. https://doi.org /10.1016/j.respol.2018.02.009.

Lockett, A. L., Ruiz, I. D., Sanchez, J. C. & Carter, C. (2021). *Race, rhetoric, and research methods.* The WAC Clearinghouse; University Press of Colorado. https:// doi.org/10.37514/PER-B.2021.1206.

Loewenstein, G. (1996). Out of control: Visceral influences on behavior. *Organizational Behavior and Human Decision Processes, 65*(3), 272–292. https://doi.org /10.1006/obhd.1996.0028.

Lorde, A.(1983). "There is no hierarchy of oppressions." *Bulletin: Homophobia and Education.* Council on Interracial Books for Children.

Loxley, J. (2007). *Performativity.* Routledge. https://doi.org/10.4324/9780203391280.

Mack, K. M., Winter, K. & Soto, M. (Eds.). (2019). *Culturally responsive strategies for reforming STEM higher education: Turning the TIDES on inequity.* Emerald Publishing. https://doi.org/10.1108/9781787434059.

Man, J. P., Weinkauf, J. G., Tsang, M. & Sin, J. H. D. D. (2004). Why do some countries publish more than others? An international comparison of research funding, English proficiency and publication output in highly ranked general medical journals. *European Journal of Epidemiology, 19*(8), 811–817. https://doi.org/10.1023 /b:ejep.0000036571.00320.b8.

Mason, C. L., Kahle, J. B. & Gardner, A. L. (1991). Draw-a-scientist test: Future implications. *School Science and Mathematics, 91*(5), 193–198. https://doi.org/10 .1111/j.1949-8594.1991.tb12078.x.

McGee, E. O. (2020). *Black, Brown, bruised: How racialized STEM education stifles innovation.* Harvard Education Press.

McGee E. O. & Robinson, W. H. (Eds.). *Diversifying STEM: Multidisciplinary perspectives on race and gender.* Rutgers University Press.

McIntosh, P. (1989). White privilege: Unpacking the invisible knapsack. *Peace and Freedom,* July/August.

McKibben, S. (2020). Turn and talk/"Antiracist" grading starts with you. *Educational leadership, 78*(1). https://www.ascd.org/el/articles/turn-and-talk-antiracist -grading-starts-with-you.

McMullin E. (1982). Values in science. *PSA: Proceedings of the biennial meeting of the philosophy of science association, 1982*(2), 3–28. https://doi.org/10.1086 /psaprocbienmeetp.1982.2.192409.

Mead, M. & Métraux, R. (1957). The image of the scientist among high-school students: A pilot study. *Science, 126*(3270), 384–390. https://doi.org/10.1126/science .126.3270.384.

Medway, P. (2002). Fuzzy genres and community identities: The case of architecture students' sketchbooks. In R. Coe, L. Lingard & T. Teslenko (Eds.), *The rhetoric and ideology of genre: Strategies for stability and change* (pp. 123–153). Hampton Press.

Middendorf, J. & Pace, D. (2004). Decoding the disciplines: A model for helping students learn disciplinary ways of thinking. *New Directions for Teaching and Learning, 98*, 1–12. https://doi.org/10.1002/tl.142.

Miller, D. I., Nolla, K. M., Eagly, A. H. & Uttal, D. H. (2018). The development of children's gender-science stereotypes: A meta-analysis of 5 decades of U.S. draw-a-scientist studies. *Child Development, 89*(6), 1943–1955. https://doi.org/10.1111/cdev.13039.

Moghaddam, F. M. & Harré, R. (2010). Words, conflicts, and political processes. In F. M. Moghaddam & R. Harré, (Eds.), *Words of conflict, words of war: How the language we use in political processes sparks fighting* (pp. 1–27). Praeger.

Moje, E. B., Ciechanowski, K. M., Kramer, K., Ellis, L., Carrillo, R. & Collazo, T. (2004). Working toward third space in content area literacy: An examination of everyday funds of knowledge and Discourse. *Reading Research Quarterly, 39*(1), 38–70. https://doi.org/10.1598/RRQ.39.1.4.

Moje, E. B., Collazo, T., Carrillo, R. & Marx, R. W. (2001). "Maestro, what is 'quality'?": Language, literacy, and discourse in project-based science. *Journal of Research in Science Teaching, 38*(4), 469–498. https://doi.org/10.1002/tea.1014.

Moll, L. C. & González, N. (1994). Lessons from research with language-minority children. *Journal of Literacy Research, 26*(4), 439–456. https://doi.org/10.1080/10862969409547862.

Morning, A. (2008). Reconstructing race in science and society: Biology textbooks, 1952–2002. *American Journal of Sociology, 114*(S1), S106–S137. https://doi.org/10.1086/592206.

Mountford, R. (2001). On gender and rhetorical space. *Rhetoric Society Quarterly, 31*(1), 41–71. https://doi.org/10.1080/02773940109391194.

Nathan, M. J., Alibali, M. W. & Koedinger, K. R. (n.d.). *Expert blind spot: When content knowledge and pedagogical content knowledge collide* (Technical report 00–05). University of Colorado, Boulder, Institute of Cognitive Science. https://www.colorado.edu/ics/sites/default/files/attached-files/00-05.pdf.

National Center for Science and Engineering Statistics. (n.d.). *Table 1. Federal obligations for science and engineering to universities and colleges, by type of activity: FY 1963–2009 (Dollars in thousands)*. National Science Foundation. Retrieved October 10, 2022, from http://www.nsf.gov/statistics/nsf13303/pdf/tab01.pdf.

National Center for Science and Engineering Statistics. (2015, June 29). *Scientific and engineering research facilities at college and universities: 1998*. National Science Foundation, Division of Science Resources Study. https://wayback.archive-it.org/5902/20150629135329/http://www.nsf.gov/statistics/nsf01301/c7.htm.

National Center for Science and Engineering Statistics. (2019, March 8). *Table 5-3: Bachelor's degrees awarded, by field, citizenship, ethnicity, and race: 2006–16*. National Science Foundation. https://ncses.nsf.gov/pubs/nsf19304/assets/data/tables/wmpd19-sr-tab05-004.pdf.

National Research Council. (2000). *How people learn: Brain, mind, experience, and school* (expanded ed.). National Academy Press. https://doi.org/10.17226/9853.

Office of Institutional Research. (2015, March). *Fall 2014 fact book* (OIR 15–07). John Jay College of Criminal Justice. http://www.jjay.cuny.edu/sites/default/files/con tentgroups/instu_research_assessment/FACT_BOOK_2014.pdf.

Oh, S. S., Galanter, J., Thakur, N., Pino-Yanes, M., Barcelo, N. E., White, M. J., de Bruin, D. M., Greenblatt, R. M., Bibbins-Domingo, K., Wu, A.H.B., Borrell, L. N., Gunter, C., Powe, N. R. & Burchard, E. G. (2015). Diversity in clinical and biomedical research: A promise yet to be fulfilled. *PLoS Medicine, 12*(12), Article e1001918. https://doi.org/10.1371/journal.pmed.1001918.

Ong, M. (2005). Body projects of young women of color in physics: Intersections of gender, race, and science. *Social Problems, 52*(4), 593–617. https://doi.org/10.1525/sp.2005.52.4.593.

Ong, M., Smith, J. M. and Ko, L. T. (2018). Counterspaces for women of color in STEM higher education: Marginal and central spaces for persistence and success. *Journal of Research in Science Teaching, 55*(2), 206–245. https://doi.org/10.1002/tea.21417.

Ong, M., Wright, C., Espinosa, L. & Orfield, G. (2011). Inside the double bind: A synthesis of empirical research on undergraduate and graduate women of color in science, technology, engineering, and mathematics. *Harvard Educational Review, 81*(2), 172–209. https://doi.org/10.17763/haer.81.2.t022245n7x4752v2.

Perryman-Clark, S. M. & Craig, C. L. (2019). *Black perspectives in writing program administration: From the margins to the center.* Conference on College Composition and Communication of the National Council of Teachers of English.

Pierce, C. (1974). Psychiatric problems of the Black minority. In S. Arieti & K. H. Brodie (Eds.), *American Handbook of Psychiatry: Advances and New Directions* (2nd ed., vol. 7, pp. 512–523). Basic Books.

Plevkova, J., Brozmanova, M., Harsanyiova, J., Sterusky, M., Honetschlager, J. & Buday, T. (2020). Various aspects of sex and gender bias in biomedical research. *Physiological research, 69*(Suppl 3), S367–S378. https://doi.org/10.33549/physiolres.934593.

Poe, M. (2013). Re-framing race in teaching writing across the curriculum. *Across the Disciplines, 10*(3). https://doi.org/10.37514/ATD-J.2013.10.3.06.

Poe, M., Inoue, A. B. & Elliott, N. (Eds.). (2018). *Writing assessment, social justice, and the advancement of opportunity.* The WAC Clearinghouse; University Press of Colorado. https://doi.org/10.37514/PER-B.2018.0155.

Pratt, M. L. (1991). Arts of the contact zone. *Profession,* 33–40. https://www.jstor.org/stable/25595469.

Primack, R. B., Ellwood, E., Miller-Rushing, A. J., Marrs, R. & Mulligan, A. (2009). Do gender, nationality, or academic age affect review decisions? An analysis of submissions to the journal *Biological Conservation. Biological Conservation, 142*(11), 2415–2418. https://doi.org/10.1016/j.biocon.2009.06.021.

Program for Research Initiatives in Science and Math. (2016). *Admission Requirements.* Retrieved from https://web.archive.org/web/20160327101547/http://pris matjjay.org/for-inquiring-minds/admission-requirements/.

Rabelo, V. C., Robotham, K. J. & McCluney, C. L. (2021). "Against a sharp white background": How Black women experience the white gaze at work. *Gender, Work and Organization, 28*(5), 1840–1858. https://doi.org/10.1111/gwao.12564.

Ramírez, D. A. (2017). *Medical imagery and fragmentation: Modernism, scientific discourse, and the Mexican/Indigenous body, 1870–1940s.* Lexington Books.

Reiff, M. J. & Bawarshi, A. (2011). Tracing discursive resources: How students use prior genre knowledge to negotiate new writing contexts in first-year composition. *Written Communication, 28*(3), 312–337. https://doi.org/10.1177/07410883 11410183.

Royster, J. J. & Williams, J. C. (1999). History in the spaces left: African American presence and narratives of composition studies. *College Composition and Communication, 50*(4), 563–584. https://library.ncte.org/journals/CCC/issues /v50-4/1348.

Rudick, C. K. & Golsan, K. B. (2018). Civility and White institutional presence: An exploration of White students' understanding of race-talk at a traditionally White institution. *Howard Journal of Communication, 29*(4), 335–352. https://doi.org/10.1 080/10646175.2017.1392910.

Ruiz, I. D. (2016). *Reclaiming composition for Chicano/as and other ethnic minorities: A critical history and pedagogy.* Palgrave Macmillan. https://doi.org/10.1057 /978-1-137-53673-0.

Ruiz, I. & Baca, D. (2017). Decolonial options and writing studies. *Composition Studies, 45*(2), 226–229. https://www.jstor.org/stable/26402796.

Ruttan, R. L., McDonnell, M.-H. & Nordgren, L. F. (2015). Having "been there" doesn't mean I care: When prior experience reduces compassion for emotional distress. *Journal of Personality and Social Psychology, 108*(4), 610–622. https://doi .org/10.1037/pspi0000012.

Saldaña, J. (2015). *The coding manual for qualitative researchers* (3rd ed.). SAGE.

Samayoa, A. C. (2018). "People around me here, they know the struggle": Students' experiences with faculty member's mentorship at three Hispanic serving institutions. *Education Sciences, 8*(2), Article 49. https://doi.org/10.3390/educsci8020049.

Saunders, M. & Serna, I. (2004). Making college happen: The college experiences of first-generation Latino students. *Journal of Hispanic Higher Education, 3*(2), 146–163. https://doi.org/10.1177%2F1538192703262515.

Searle, J. R. (1969). *Speech acts: An essay in the philosophy of language.* Cambridge University Press. https://doi.org/10.1017/CBO9781139173438.

Seymour, E. & Hewitt, N. M. (1997). *Talking about leaving: Why undergraduates leave the sciences.* Westview Press.

Shor, I. (1986). *Culture wars: School and society in the conservative restoration 1969–1984.* Routledge and Kegan Paul.

Sims, J. J. (2018). *Revolutionary STEM education: Critical-reality pedagogy and social justice in STEM for Black males.* Peter Lang.

Smit, D. W. (2004). *The end of composition studies.* Southern Illinois University Press.

Smith, B. (Ed.). (2000). *Home girls: A Black feminist anthology.* Rutgers University Press.

Smitherman, G. (1986). *Talkin and testifyin: The language of Black America.* Wayne State University Press.

Soja, E. W. (1996). *Thirdspace: Journeys to Los Angeles and other real-and-imagined places.* Blackwell.

Solórzano, D., Ceja, M & Yosso, T. (2000). Critical race theory, racial microaggressions, and campus racial climate: The experiences of African American college students. *The Journal of Negro Education,* 69(1/2), 60–73. https://www.jstor.org/stable/2696265.

Solorzano, D. G. & Delagdo Bernal, D. (2001). Examining transformational resistance through a critical race and Latcrit theory framework: Chicana and Chicano students in an urban context. *Urban Education,* 36(3), 308–342. https://doi.org/10.1177%2F0042085901363002.

Solórzano, D. G. & Yosso, T. J. (2002). Critical race methodology: Counter-storytelling as an analytical framework for education research. *Qualitative Inquiry,* 8(1), 23–44. https://doi.org/10.1177%2F107780040200800103.

Sommers, N. & Saltz, L. (2004). The novice as expert: Writing the freshman year. *College Composition and Communication,* 56(1), 124–149. https://library.ncte.org/journals/CCC/issues/v56-1/3993.

Spellmeyer, K. (1998). "Too Little Care": Language, politics, and embodiment in the life-world. In M. Bernard-Donals & R. R. Glejzer (Eds.), *Rhetoric in an antifoundational world: Language, culture, and pedagogy* (pp. 254–291). Yale University Press.

Stake, R. E. (1981). Case study methodology: An epistemological advocacy. In W. W. Welsh (Ed.), *Case study methodology in educational evaluation. Proceedings of the 1981 Minnesota Evaluation Conference* (pp. 31–40). Minnesota Research and Evaluation Center.

Street, B. (2001). The new literacy studies. In E. Cushman, E. R. Kintgen, B. M. Kroll & M. Rose (Eds.), *Literacy: A critical sourcebook* (pp. 430–442). Bedford/St. Martin's.

Sue, D. W. (2010). *Microaggressions in everyday life: Race, gender, and sexual orientation.* Wiley.

Sue, D. W., Capodilupo, C. M., Torino, G. C., Bucceri, J. M., Holder, A.M.B., Nadal, K. L. & Esquilin, M. (2007). Racial microaggressions in everyday life: Implications for clinical practice. *American Psychologist,* 62(4), 271–286. https://doi.org/10.1037/0003-066x.62.4.271.

Swales, J. (1990). *Genre analysis: English in academic and research settings.* Cambridge University Press.

Tajfel, H. & Turner, J. C. (1979). An integrative theory of intergroup conflict. In W. G. Austin & S. Worchel (Eds.), *The social psychology of intergroup relations* (pp. 33–37). Brooks/Cole Publishing.

Tate, W. F. (1997). Critical race theory and education: History, theory, and implications. *Review of Research in Education,* 22(1), 195–247. https://doi.org/10.3102%2F0091732X022001195.

Thomas, P. L. (2017, May 30). *Power, responsibility, and the white men of Academia.* HuffPost. https://www.huffpost.com/entry/power-responsibility-and-the-white-men-of-academia_b_592d58bce4b08861edoccbce.

Tinto, V. (1993). *Leaving college: Rethinking the causes and cures of student attrition* (2nd ed.). University of Chicago Press.

Torres, L. E. (2013). Lost in the numbers: Gender equity discourses and women of color in science, technology, engineering and mathematics (STEM). *The International Journal of Science in Society*, 3(4), 33–46. https://doi.org/10.18848/1836-6236 /CGP/v03i04/51352.

United Nations University. (2015, July 13). *Rom Harré Positioning Theory Symposium Bruges 8 July 2105* [Video]. YouTube. https://www.youtube.com/watch?v=CxmH Tk7aYto.

Anonymous High School (2017). Mission statement. Anonymous High School.

van den Brink, M. & Benschop, Y. (2012). Gender practices in the construction of academic excellence: Sheep with five legs. *Organization*, 19(4), 507–524. https:// doi.org/10.1177%2F1350508411414293.

van den Brink, M. & Benschop, Y. (2014). Gender in academic networking: The role of gatekeepers in professorial recruitment. *Journal of Management Studies*, 51(3), 460–492. https://doi.org/10.1111/joms.12060.

Vargas, N. (2018). Racial expropriation in higher education: Are Whiter Hispanic serving institutions more likely to receive minority serving institution funds? *Socius: Sociological Research for a Dynamic World*, 4. https://doi.org/10.1177 %2F2378023118794077.

Vargas, N. & Villa-Palomino, J. (2019). Racing to serve or race-ing for money? Hispanic-serving institutions and the colorblind allocation of racialized federal funding. *Sociology of Race and Ethnicity*, 5(3), 401–415. https://doi.org/10.1177 %2F2332649218769409.

Vasconcelos, S.M.R., Sorenson, M. M., Leta, J., Sant'Ana, M. C. & Batista, P. D. (2008). Researchers' writing competence: A bottleneck in the publication of Latin-American science? *EMBO Reports*, 9(8), 700–702. https://doi.org/10.1038%2 Fembor.2008.143.

Vavrus, M. (2008). Culturally responsive teaching. In T. Good (Ed.), *21st century education: A reference handbook* (vol. 2), pp. 49–57. SAGE Publications.

Villanueva, V., Jr. (1993). *Bootstraps: From an American academic of color.* National Council of Teachers of English.

Vygotsky, L. S. (1978). *Mind in society: The development of higher psychological processes.* Harvard University Press.

Walton, R., Moore, K. R., and Jones, N. N. (2019). *Technical communication after the social justice turn: Building coalitions for action.* Routledge. https://doi.org/10.4324 /9780429198748.

Wenger, E. (1998). *Communities of practice: Learning, meaning, and identity.* Cambridge University Press. https://doi.org/10.1017/CBO9780511803932.

Whitcomb, K. M., Kalender, Z. Y., Nokes-Malach, T. J., Schunn, C. D. & Singh, C. (2020). Engineering students' performance in foundational courses as a predictor of future academic success. *The International Journal of Engineering Education*, 36(4), 1340–1355. https://www.ijee.ie/latestissues/Vol36-4/20_ijee3956.pdf.

Wilder, L. (2012). *Rhetorical strategies and genre conventions in literary studies: Teaching and writing in the disciplines.* Southern Illinois University Press.

Winsor, D. A. (1996). *Writing like an engineer: A rhetorical education.* Lawrence Erlbaum Associates.

Yager, R. E. & Yager. S. O. (1985). Changes in the perceptions of science for third, seventh, and eleventh grade students. *Journal of Research in Science Teaching,* 22(4), 347–358. https://doi.org/10.1002/tea.366022040.

Young, V. A., Barret, R, Young-Rivera, Y & Lovejoy, K. B. (2018). *Other people's English: Code-meshing, code-switching, and African American literacy.* Parlor Press.

Appendix. Methodological and Analytical Procedures

I have thought of the primary audience for this book as one of educators and administrators interested in making STEM spaces more accessible and equitable for students from historically minoritized backgrounds. For this reason, I have not approached the data presentation or analysis in the way one might traditionally handle an empirical study; my research methods and analytical approach have taken a backseat to the student voices and experiences. It is understandable, however, that readers may be interested in a deeper understanding of my methods— how I collected and analyzed data and how I validated the information presented.

What follows is a discussion of how I selected participants, how I engaged with them in data collection over time, and how I analyzed that data once acquired. It is important to note that, though this was not a study that used participatory action research methods—meaning, students were not co-researchers and did not have a hand in the study design—ethically, I felt it was important to "clear" my written interpretations of those student and mentor experiences early and often. As a first step in the writing up of my findings, I composed individual case study chapters for each student participant that chronicled their time in the program and the observations that I made in light of my research questions. I gave those individual chapters to each student participant to read and comment on and to correct any misconceptions or add additional insight. Only in the case of Ruben, who told his mentor Dr. Martinez he was participating, was a chapter member-checked with a mentor. I had the other mentors member-check my analytical memos. In two instances, mentors declined to engage in member-checking but gave approval to move forward.

In writing this book, I drew heavily on those individual case study drafts to answer my research questions. I strategically chose not to present any data that would reveal participants' identities, except in the case where approval was granted. As a result, many of the written artifacts from the study are not directly presented but are rather discussed in a way to preserve anonymity.

Participant Selection

In August 2015, I received IRB approval from both the Research Foundation of CUNY (IRB#2015-0770) and Northeastern University (IRB#15-09-16). At that time, I emailed the 27 mentors associated with PRISM to introduce the research project and ask if I might speak to them about participating. After introductory conversations, ten mentors agreed to participate (consent was both verbal and written, per IRB); initial data collection consisted of a one-hour semi-structured interview about the mentors' own experiences learning to read and write as scientists, their writing processes, and their pedagogical approaches in the class-room and laboratory. It is important to note that not all mentors interviewed had students participating in this project, and not all student participants had mentors participating. Data from the larger group of mentors, however, provided important insights about the administration of the program as a whole and about the culture and inclusiveness of the individual laboratories.

At the end of August 2015, I attended PRISM's three-day research training workshop, a required activity for any student wishing to pursue undergraduate research in the program. At that workshop, I introduced myself to the 12 students who attended and anonymously collected their perceptions on the discourse community of science through group discussion that was recorded. I subsequently emailed each student who had participated asking them if they would like to take part in the research (offering a $25 gift card to a major online retailer as incentive). Two students agreed (verbal and written consent were obtained), and I conducted initial audio-recorded interviews in Autumn 2015. In January 2016, I repeated that process with the newest cohort of research students, and I repeated it again in August 2016 and May 2017. A total of 11 students began participation in the study, with five withdrawing at various points due to time constraints for some and due to withdrawing from PRISM for others.

Because the focus of this research is on women and BIPOC students partici-pating in a URE in science, I was deliberate in participant selection—I recruited only from enrolled PRISM students, who are predominantly female and BIPOC. I screened participants for age: only those 18 years old and older were accepted as participants. I did not screen for any other social factors (i.e., socioeconomic class). Also, because the project focuses on development, I intentionally recruited only those students who were just entering the program, often before they had connected with a mentor. In this way, I was able to follow them from their starts in the program, through multiple semesters as undergraduate researchers (includ-ing summer externships), and in some cases to graduation.

Data Collection

The data collected for this study included

- 15 hours of semi-structured interviews with mentors,
- 35 hours of semi-structured interviews with the six student participants,
- 32 drafts of student research proposals and ten poster drafts (where applicable),
- individualized proposal feedback from mentors and program staff,
- analytical memos and direct observation of program training workshops, and
- an assortment of textual artifacts produced or read by the student infor-mants (e.g., lab notes).

Data collection involved conducting a preliminary one-hour interview with students before (or just at the start of) their URE, then conducting subsequent 45-minute interviews after they submitted research proposals, at the end of each semester, and in some cases at the point of graduation. On average, this process provided me with check-ins with students once every three months, a long enough span of time for some development to occur but not so long that the students would not be able to recall their experiences in the intervals between interviews. All interviews were semi-structured and largely student-driven,[10] allowing them to develop confidence and us to develop rapport.

I also asked students to save and share with me copies of all research proposals and (where applicable) presentation and poster drafts, including mentor feedback. Where multiple drafts were unavailable (i.e., because a student misplaced a paper file), I posed detailed interview questions about the mentor feedback to both the students and mentors. The level of detail in the recall by students was particularly impressive. In some instances, I collected as referents additional written materials from students, such as laboratory notebooks, papers written for class, and personal notes. While student-mentor phone texts and emails were not available for direct analysis, I also posed interview questions about this material.

I conducted interviews with mentors and administrative staff less frequently than with students. To ensure confidentiality, neither mentors nor staff were made aware of student participation, and vice versa. In one case, a student self-disclosed to their mentor during the study. In that case, after being given permission, I asked the mentor specific questions about the student. Where this was not the case, I asked mentors specific questions about *all* the PRISM students within their laboratory. Since feedback from the program coordinators was also an important pedagogical element, I requested the written feedback they provided on documents for *all* students and parsed these afterward, and my interviews with the coordinators focused on the program as a whole rather than on individual students.

During the four-year period this study covers, I was also able to observe three training workshops (two in person, one virtually) offered by the research program, as well as three annual program symposia in which students publicly presented their research in poster sessions. This provided me an opportunity to observe their public speaking skills. Though direct observation of the students in their everyday laboratory practices was an initial goal in data collection, in the end this was not possible due to conflicting student schedules and the odd hours students worked in the lab (i.e., from 8:00 to 10:00 pm on weekday evenings and on weekends). Further, from interviews I learned that students rarely worked alongside their mentors in the laboratory; rather, they checked in via email or text and met for weekly or

---

10. By "student-driven," I mean that I pursued what students seemed most interested in discussing at a given moment, connecting back to my research interests as appropriate. This allowed for richer data and also made for much more natural conversation.

monthly laboratory meetings for updates. As such, direct observation of mentoring was not an option. Direct observation of laboratory meetings was also not an option because mentors felt this would be too disruptive.

Data Analysis

My analysis of the data was ongoing and recursive. As Richard E. Boyatzis (1998) notes, "[the] type of information collected both affects and is affected by the unit of analysis" (p. 63); thus, identifying early what the primary aims of the project were and the ways to address those aims was critical. Since student experiences and writing development were at the focus of this study, I decided that my primary unit of analysis would be the individual students themselves because they are "the entity on which the interpretation of the study will focus" (Boyatzis, 1998, p. 62). This decision was methodologically congruent with my selection of the case study approach and led to the selection of appropriate, relevant data streams. As such, I determined two primary units of coding per participant: the student interviews and the student writing.

Student Interviews

From the very start of the project, I transcribed interviews within a day or two of recording them, and I blinded materials as I went to ensure informant anonymity. In the first interview, I asked student participants to suggest their own pseudonyms, and those were used for tracking. Using my research questions as a loose referent, I *initially* coded[11] these interviews inductively, using my interpretation of what was occurring on the page—for example, when a student spoke explicitly about genre or discourse conventions. I conducted this initial step to organize the data and identify preliminary themes (i.e., genre awareness, sense of belonging) across the participants as well as across time. During this process, I identified potential *in situ* codes (such as "the young Padawan" to describe a student's status in the science discipline) as well as quotations that seemed particularly significant to the research questions at hand. This initial step allowed me to see that certain themes surrounding identity and development were present, for example the influence of mentor expectations and "rules" on student confidence and self-efficacy.

Subsequent to this first step, I determined that using my research questions as a more specific referent (i.e., "prior genre knowledge," "mentor expectations") was an efficient way to organize the interview data and that identity-related codes (e.g., "positive identity association") were useful in understanding the level of

---

11. I did all coding by hand, on paper, rather that digitally. Not only was this approach more in line with my own work style, it allowed me to see, spatially, the changes that took place over time.

affinity the student may or may not have felt with the scientific community at a given time. I coded interviews in batches by student to allow for focus on the individual's experience and development over time.

Student Writing

Rhetorical analysis was the primary method I used to analyze student writing. I assessed the students' use of rhetorical devices to determine the proximity of student writing to scientific discourse conventions. I coded proposals and other textual artifacts produced by students for rhetorical conventions of scientific discourse, using Ken Hyland's (2005 & 2012) and Swales' (1990) work as referents. This analysis included noting changes between revisions and involved the consideration of tone, point of view, use of jargon, rhetorical conventions, and genre conventions.

I also examined feedback from mentors and staff members, looking for pedagogical moments and for their reconciliation with scientific discourse conventions. I used as referents for coding for context descriptors of strong scientific writing provided in interviews by mentors and staff members, since mentors and staff members were the ultimate evaluative audience for (and instructors of) the writing artifacts students provided. I also took into account tone of feedback and clarity of instruction.

Finally, I identified intertextual and interdiscursive elements (what broad, social currents were affecting the text; how individuals were being positioned in the laboratory or in their science disciplines broadly). I used the results of this multi-dimensional approach to triangulate with student and mentor interviews in order to explore my research questions.

Analytical Approach

The overarching, guiding foci for this study—understanding the ways in which students from underrepresented backgrounds in STEM education negotiated disciplinary discourse conventions in a URE and the impacts of those negotiations on scientific identities—are complex ones. In pursuing these lines of inquiry, what I have been interested in discovering is how women and BIPOC students learn to present themselves as scientists in written and spoken discourse and how their reading and listening practices change to be more or less in line with the practices of professional scientists. Importantly, I have been focused on the role social factors like race/ethnicity, gender, and socioeconomic class play in this development. To answer these larger queries, I broke out sub-questions that would help elucidate different facets. While not all of these questions are answered directly in this book, they all aided in helping me answer the questions identified in the Introduction: How do the norms and expectations of higher education and STEM, specifically, impact the development of scientific identity and discursive skill? What role do societal markers like race and gender play in the negotiation of identity in STEM learning environments? What follows is a description of the analytical approach I took in attempting to answer each of these questions.

How Is Disciplinary Discursive Development Mediated by Prior Knowledge?

In this research, I used the term "mediation" to refer to the influence of various factors on disciplinary identity and writing development. In this sub-question, for example, I was interested in how students' prior knowledge with science, writing, reading, etc., might affect the ways in which they present themselves as scientists. Drawing on the work of Mary Jo Reiff and Anis Bawarshi (2011), I approached this sub-question by asking the following questions:

- What experiences with reading and writing scientific materials do students report having had prior to joining PRISM?
- Which scientific genres are noted, and what associations (positive, negative, or neutral) do students report having with those genres?

Because this project is deeply connected to agency and identity, I also asked,

- What relevant educational experiences do students report having before becoming a student at the college and before becoming an undergraduate researcher?
- What identities have been applied to students prior to joining the program by family, community, and education professionals?

Prior to analyzing the student interviews, I prepared by brainstorming the ways in which answers to these questions might show up in the data: students might have reported having had a high school experience that was very focused on STEM disciplines (i.e., at a magnet or charter school) or having grown up with scientists (chemists, doctors, pharmacists, etc.) in their family. I also noted that I might find the opposite: students reporting limited exposure to science coursework before college or having grown up with family that had a distrust of science or that questioned its viability as a career. In terms of reading and writing skill, it was important to know how students identified with the acts of reading and writing (as well as speaking and listening) as they entered the program. Had they adopted an identity as a "strong reader" or "bookworm"? Had they been told by others that they were academically gifted or challenged?

In the case of this sub-question, I was interested in learning not just what students knew about *science* before entering the program, but also what they knew about *themselves*. When reviewing and coding transcripts, I looked for moments when students talked about how they came to the program, what sorts of experiences they had with regard to science as a discipline, how they saw themselves as readers and writers, what their perceived ideas were about the kind of reading and writing scientists do, and what they considered "good" scientific writing.

As Reiff and Bawarshi (2011) noted in their research into the influence of prior knowledge on genre transfer, relying "on students' *reported* cognitive processes and retrospective reflections has its limitations" (p. 317). Like them, I was cautious in my analysis because students are not always aware of their skill level, their transfer of knowledge from one space to another, or even the social circumstances that have helped construct their identities. At the same time, I knew that the lived experience of the students—*what they believed about themselves* as they entered the program—would be paramount to understanding their development of discursive skill and scientific identity over time.

Prior knowledge also had direct implications for the other sub-questions I explored. It affects genre, mentoring, cultural considerations, and program expectations and requirements. I used this interweaving to the study's benefit by using the prior knowledge question to address elements of the other four. I was able to identity the scientific genres each student had exposure to prior to joining PRISM, for example, including both macrogenre types (such as article summaries) and situated rhetorical genres (such as abstracts and scientific posters). This was important because, in terms of identity work, the different genres serve very different purposes. Summaries allow a student to demonstrate comprehension and knowledge of difficult scientific content, while abstracts allow a student to demonstrate knowledge of the discourse conventions of the discipline. One speaks to content, while the other speaks to form. Some students excel in one form (e.g., summaries) because it allows for rhetorical leniency, while others excel in other forms (e.g., proposals) because of their strict language rules and perceived formulaic, plug-and-play structure.

How are Scientific Writing and Identity Development Mediated by Mentors and Mentoring?

The influence of mentors on the scientific identity and discursive development of these students was also of importance. Mentors—primarily faculty, but also peer—play critical roles in students' research and practical science education. They also have varying approaches to teaching the reading and writing practices of professional scientists. While every individual's reading and writing process is different, the end results must conform to the discourse community's expectations if the work is to be seen as credible. Thus, the bar I set for defining "professional" level writing was that of the scientific community's expectations on style, genre, tone, etc.

For this question, I was interested in learning how the mentors' instructional styles (e.g., explicit genre instruction) as well as their requirements and expectations (even their own writing styles) assisted or restrained student development of the discursive practices of the scientific community. This involved identifying how mentors guided students in the proposal, poster, lab notebook, etc., writing processes, as well as in presentation preparation. Reading was also important, so

I examined the ways in which mentors explicitly or implicitly taught their students how to read scientific material. As I engaged with the various data streams, I consistently asked,

- How are mentors cultivating scientific identity in their students?
- What *kind* of scientific identity, if any, are mentors cultivating?
- How involved are mentors in instruction about scientific reading, writing, speaking, and listening practices for their students?
- What does that instruction *look* like?

These data largely came from interviews with both mentors and students but also arose from examinations of textual artifacts for comments and modeling of discourse conventions. From prior experience with the program, I knew that there were widely disparate approaches to mentoring and to discourse instruction particularly. There was a wide continuum in approaches to instruction, and I was interested in learning what effect these might have on students' own discursive and reported scientific identities. As such, when examining both student and mentor interviews, I looked for moments when either spoke about the mentor's reported approach (or actual practices) with students in the lab. This included how mentors spoke to their students, their expectations for language use, documentation procedures, and other activities that constitute the *being* of a scientist. In examining textual artifacts, I similarly looked for moments when mentors explicitly or implicitly instructed students in the discursive practices of scientists as well as looked for "teaching moments" that were *not* taken up.

How is Disciplinary Discourse Development Mediated by Scientific Genres?

Much of the communal discourse in science takes place through specific scientific genres: research proposals and reports, scientific articles and brevia, etc. In order for individuals to be recognized by other scientists *as* scientists, their successful engagement with and performance of scientific genres is critical. In posing this question, I was interested in discovering how the students engaged with different scientific genres and whether success or failure in one influenced success or failure in another. For example, if students wrote literature reviews as part of their early research, did that help them in their first proposal writing process? Also, how did their experience with writing in a genre change over time? Did the proposals get stronger semester to semester? Stay the same?

How is Disciplinary Discourse Development Mediated by Program Requirements and Expectations?

As an undergraduate research program, PRISM instituted various requirements and expectations (both explicit and implicit) for students. Explicitly, students must have been majoring in forensic science, computer science, or cell and molecular biology, as well as have possessed *some* interest in an advanced degree. Before partnering with a lab, students were required to attend the research training workshop, where they discussed scientific ethics, conduct, and professional and community responsibility, as well as more practical aspects of scientific methods, such as literature searching, record keeping, report writing, and basic laboratory techniques/protocols.

Though institutional factors could have been a study unto themselves, by focusing on program requirements and expectations in this sub-question, I was interested in exploring whether the requirements and expectations of the program itself—not the mentors—influenced the students' discursive identities. In exploring this question, I needed to pay close attention to the ways in which students spoke of engaging with the various deadlines, samples, and procedures of the program, asking of the data the following:

- In what ways, if any, does the way *staff enforcement* of genre requirements (i.e., proposals, posters, abstracts) influence the ways students write/approach the documents?
- Do students see the research proposal as simply a hurdle to be jumped or as a heuristic for their research process?
- How do program requirements influence the ways in which students present themselves discursively?
- Are program expectations reasonable and clearly identifiable by students?

How Are Scientific Writing and Identity Development Mediated by Race, Gender, Socioeconomic Status, and/or other Societal Markers?

How people approach an identity is influenced by that identity's prevalence in our culture. Science-related fields are typically perceived as fields that pay well; thus, socioeconomic factors play a role in whether an individual sees a science-related career as a viable career path. Science disciplines are also predominantly White and male; thus, underrepresentation influences how members of underrepresented communities approach those disciplines (National Center for Science and Engineering Statistics, 2015). Since STEM fields are also often perceived as "sterile," free from human emotion, and place where only measurable proof has value (as described by students in this study), entering these spaces can likewise present conflicts for those who have deeply rooted religious beliefs or draw on ways of knowing that do not conform with traditional STEM ontology. Thus, when considering this question, I was looking to see if and when issues of gender, race/ethnicity, religion, socioeconomic status, or any other societal marker became salient in the data, and if is, if those issues influenced whether or not students engaged with or successfully took up the conventions of scientific discourse. Part of this question also connects to students' future career intentions, as that is at least in part a socioeconomic factor. Students' motivation for getting into a science-related field also presented useful information for exploring this question.

Given the context of the institution (an HSI and MSI), as well as the social circumstances in which this research was taking place (i.e., during the 2016 presidential election and subsequent administration in which race and gender issues were prominent), I sought to identify ways in which these historically underrepresented individuals embraced, pushed against, and/or disrupted the rhetoric of science, both as an embodied practice and as a discursive one. To that end, I regularly posed questions of culture and social factors, with an eye toward answering the following:

- How do students perceive the community and culture of science disciplines before, during, and after their URE?
- In what ways are gender, race/ethnicity, religion, socioeconomic status, or other cultural identifiers embraced, rejected, or ignored during the URE?
- Are any cultural identifiers absorbed as part of these students' discursive identities as scientists and, if so, how are they made apparent?

Analytical Method

Throughout this study, after each interview with a student or mentor, I composed analytical memos to describe what I thought I was hearing come out of the conversations as related to my research questions. These memos included notes about tone of voice, such as whether speakers were assertive or hesitant in their discussions of particular topics, as well as ideas the conversation made me think about. I referred to these memos later during my analysis of transcripts and written artifacts, asking myself whether what I noticed held up against the data. In subsequent interviews with the students and mentors, I often brought up the observations noted in my memos to ask participants whether what I noticed was accurate or off base. In this way, my analytical method was recursive and reflexive throughout.